1000 Finn Wolfhard Facts

Mera Wolfe

Contents

PREFACE

Think you know everything there is to know about about Finn Wolfhard? Well, think again. The book which follows contains all you could ever wish to know about this young superstar. Facts about Stranger Things, fashion, music, likes & dislikes, food, career, background, movies, Calpurnia, Stephen King's IT, lifestyle, quotes, famous friends and so much more all awaits in 1000 Finn Wolfhard Facts. Finn Wolfhard is definitely one of the more enigmatic cast members in Stranger Things and admits that he could happily live without fame. Hopefully this book will provide an entertaining and insightful extended profile of Finn Wolfhard with plenty of fascinating trivia and things you didn't know.

1000 FINN WOLFHARD FACTS

(1) Finn Wolfhard was born in Vancouver, British Columbia, Canada, in 2002.

(2) Finn has a brother five years his senior.

(3) Finn is of French, German, and Jewish descent.

(4) Finn went to Catholic school.

(5) Finn's father was a screenwriter and so Finn always had an interest in acting and films. Vancouver has a thriving film and television production industry so it was perhaps almost inevitable that Finn would become an actor.

(6) Finn got his first acting gig through Craigslist.

(7) Finn said he took a summer acting class as a kid but didn't think it helped him much.

(8) Finn said he didn't like school very much because he was bullied. "Yeah, I was bullied at school. I was bullied a lot in elementary school. It's awful."

(9) Finn made his television debut as Zoran in The 100.

(10) Another of Finn's early roles was in the popular TV show Supernatural.

(11) Finn appeared in his first music video in 2012.

(12) At the time of writing, Finn has appeared in ten music videos.

(13) In 2015, Finn was cast as Richie Tozier in a film version of Stephen King's IT. Finn was cast by Cary Fukunaga - who was slated to direct IT at the time.

(14) Cary Fukunaga left the production of IT and had be replaced by another director. This meant there was a delay and during that period Finn took part in open auditions for Stranger Things. Had there not been a change of director and delay in the production of IT then Finn would never have been cast as Mike Wheeler in Stranger Things because he simply would not have been available.

"I had actually been hired to do IT before Stranger Things," said Finn. "This was when Cary Fukunaga was going to direct and then pulled out. From there I got Stranger Things."

(15) Cary Fukunaga was replaced by Andy Muschietti as the director of IT. Finn actually had to audition again for Muschietti but it went well and for the second (and thankfully final) time he was given the part of Richie Tozier. "When It came back with Andy Muschietti directing, I got the opportunity to audition again."

(16) Finn was born on the 23rd of December. That makes him a Capricorn.

(17) Stranger Things was originally titled Montauk. Montauk is a hamlet at the east end of the Long Island peninsula and famed for its beaches. Ross and Matt Duffer, the brothers who created Stranger Things, were very inspired by Steven Spielberg's classic movie Jaws in their early plans for the show.

"Jaws was our favorite movie of all time," said Matt Duffer, "so we liked the sort of coastal setting that allowed, but for production reasons it started to look more and more unfeasible."

(18) One of the main reasons why the show was originally going to be set in Montauk is Camp Hero. Camp Hero (aka Montauk Air Force Station) is an abandoned military base in Montauk which gave rise to all manner of conspiracy theories.

It was alleged in a book called The Montauk Project that Camp Hero used kidnapped children in experiments which included telekinesis and time travel. Most of the conspiracy theories involving Montauk are obviously considered to be fiction but the Duffers felt Camp Hero (with its many urban legends and alleged secrets) would be a great backdrop for a sci-fi fantasy horror show.

(19) Most of the cast in Stranger Things were hired when the show was still going to be called Montauk.

(20) Stranger Things is science fiction horror show that streams on Netflix. It is a love letter to 80s pop culture - most specifically Stephen King, Steven Spielberg, and John Carpenter. Its range of influences is vast though and takes in everything from John Hughes to Lovecraft to Clive Barker.

(21) Hundreds of boys were tested for the younger roles in Stranger Things and required to read scenes from Stand By Me and E.T. the Extra-Terrestrial in auditions.

(22) The part of Mike Wheeler was exceptionally important in season one of Stranger Things. Mike has the most lines of any character in season one and is at the heart of the story.

(23) Finn eventually won the pivotal role of Mike Wheeler despite a heavy cold which forced him to record an out of focus audition from his bed.

(24) The casting director on Stranger Things said she liked Finn because of the nervous energy he projected in his auditions. She thought this was a good fit for the character of Mike Wheeler.

(25) The Duffer Brothers said they took an instant liking to Finn because he knew a lot about eighties movies.

(26) The Duffer Brothers say that, out of the four lead boys in Stranger Things, Mike Wheeler is the most like they were at

that age.

(27) Millie Bobby Brown (who was cast as Eleven in Stranger Things) had to play scenes with various boys who were in contention to play Mike Wheeler during the casting process. When she played a scene with Finn and had excellent chemistry with him the casting department knew they had found their Mike Wheeler.

(28) In the first season of Stranger Things, Eleven is a girl with telekinetic powers who escapes from a government lab where she is held captive. Mike Wheeler and his friends Dustin and Lucas are searching for their missing friend Will Byers and find Eleven hiding in the woods. Mike secretly shelters Eleven in his basement and they learn that Eleven might be able to help them find Will.

(29) The relationship between Mike Wheeler and Eleven in season one is influenced by Tomas Alfredson's 2008 Swedish film Let the Right One In.

Let the Right One In is also set in the early eighties and concerns two eleven year-old children - a boy named Oskar and a girl named Eli - who form a close bond. Oskar is bullied at school and Eli is a vampire. As with Eleven, Eli has to stay hidden and doesn't really understand the normal mundane everyday world. Like the character of Eleven, Eli also has special powers. The Rubik's cube is an important part of the bond between the characters in Let the Right One In and we also see Mike Wheeler play with a Rubik's cube in season one of Stranger Things.

The connection between Stranger Things and Let the Right One In is confirmed when the boys pretend Eleven is their cousin from Sweden in order to smuggle her into school and use Mr Clarke's ham radio.

(30) Finn's older brother Nick is a voice actor.

(31) Finn, as a name, is not short for anything. That's his real name.

(32) Despite appearing in the movie adaptation, Finn never actually read Stephen King's novel IT. This is a famously long book. "We all tried, like, we should all do it, right?" said Finn. "And got two chapters in and thought - Yeah, it's really long, and I don't know if I have time to finish this. We also thought we should get more of an organic feel to it, so we didn't copy from the book. We tried but failed. My cousin did because she wanted to read something I was going to be in. That's dedication."

(33) Finn has a strong (and deliberate you would imagine) resemblance in season one of Stranger Things to Henry Thomas in the 1984 kids spy film Cloak & Dagger. Mike Wheeler and Davey Osborne (the character played by Henry Thomas in Cloak & Dagger) have the same hairstyle, brandish a walkie-talkie, and wear similar clothes.

(34) Finn likes to play basketball in his spare time.

(35) In season one of Stranger Things, Mike Wheeler is essentially Elliott in E.T. the Extra-Terrestrial. The Duffer Brothers had to find their own Henry Thomas.

(36) Finn has famously high cheekbones.

(37) At the time of writing, Finn is 5'11. He was obviously a lot smaller than this in the first two seasons of Stranger Things.

(38) In the pitch for Montauk (as it was called before it became Stranger Things), Mike Wheeler is described in the following way - 'Mike Wheeler is twelve. He is a cute kid, but a birthmark on his left cheek leads to much bullying and near-crippling insecurity. He has never had a first kiss, much less a girlfriend. He escapes his insecurities through reading fantasy novels, spending time with his three best friends (Lucas, Dustin, and Will), and retreating into his own vivid

imagination. The Dungeon Master of his Dungeons and Dragons group, he writes sprawling adventures with fantastical monsters. When he finds himself on a real adventure, facing real monsters, he will discover a courage he didn't know he had. By the end, he will even kiss a girl.'

(39) Finn is known for his curly hair.

(40) Finn loves frogs and launched his own frog apparel company.

(41) The pitch document for Montauk included a number of elements that were later discarded for Stranger Things. In the pitch document story notes for Montauk, Mike Wheeler ventures into the Upside Down to search for Will Byers. This never actually happened though in Stranger Things (as it became).

(42) In the pitch document, Montauk is set in the fall of 1980. The pitch proposed that the music in the show should be a synth score inspired by John Carpenter's The Fog and The Thing. It also proposed that a sequel (a second season of Montauk) would take place in 1990 when the kids are now young adults and must reunite to fight the strange forces threatening their village again. This was patently inspired by Stephen King's IT and another element in the pitch that never happened in the end.

It is sometimes reported that Montauk was pitched as an anthology show but the evidence seems to contradict this. The pitch book for Montauk clearly proposed one single story and one set of characters. The vague notion of setting a second season of the show in 1990 ten years later quickly became obsolete when Stranger Things began shooting and the Duffers saw how good the child actors were. The notion of having a second season of Strangers Things with the likes of Finn Wolfhard, Millie Bobby Brown, and Gaten Matarazzo replaced by older actors was unthinkable.

(43) The Duffers suffered many rejections when they tried to pitch Montauk (eventually to become Stranger Things) in the entertainment industry. The Duffers later said that what seemed to put people off was the fact that this proposed show had a gang of children as major characters. Network executives obviously didn't think this concept would work.

(44) Finn said he was more scared of Pennywise the Clown than the Demogorgon in Stranger Things.

(45) The first scene ever shot for Stranger Things was the first scene you see in the show - the Dungeons & Dragons game in Mike's basement.

(46) Mike Wheeler and his friends are huge fans of Dungeons & Dragons - especially in season one of stranger Things. They have marathon Dungeons & Dragons sessions in Mike's basement. Dungeons & Dragons is a roll the dice fantasy board game first released in 1974. The Duffers never played this game as children but wanted to use it as a means to convey the friendship of the boys in Stranger Things. The children in Stranger Things use Dungeons & Dragons terms to understand the strange happenings in Hawkins and this transfers as a type of shorthand to convey information to the viewer too.

(47) The game the boys are playing at the start of The Vanishing of Will Byers (which is the first ever episode of Stranger Things) foreshadows the plot of season one.

(48) Finn really dislikes bananas. "I don't like the smell or the texture. I'm not alone on that! I know it's a weird thing I have against them. I guess I'm going to have to start eating them one day, otherwise, I'll die from too little potassium or whatever."

(49) Mike Wheeler was supposed to wear an E.T - The Extra-Terrestrial watch in the first season of Stranger Things but they didn't manage to obtain the rights.

(50) When Stranger Things began production, there wasn't much buzz about the show in the online trade entertainment publications. What few reports there were tended to refer to it as the 'new Winona Ryder show'.

(51) Finn had some mint tic tacs before the scene near the end of season one of Stranger Things where Mike kisses Eleven on the cheek. He wanted to make sure his breath was super fresh.

(52) Finn said he loved the concept of Stranger Things from the start because he is a fan of retro pop culture. "The synopsis called it a love-letter to 80s teen drama, horror and sci-fi. I was like, 'I'm in.' I love retro culture. I love retro games; I love retro music. And so I was sort of in that boat from the beginning. I didn't really need any proper training."

(53) Finn said he has always been wary of clowns - so appearing in IT was no picnic.

(54) Finn has dark brown eyes.

(55) Mike Wheeler is the first character in Stranger Things to use the term the Upside Down.

(56) Finn said it was somewhat overwhelming when the first season of Stranger Things became such a phenomenon. A few times some autograph hunters followed him home - which he found quite alarming.

(57) Finn as Mike Wheeler has 433 lines in the first season of Stranger Things. This is more than any other cast member.

(58) Finn's great-great aunt was a silent film and theatre actress.

(59) It's plainly no coincidence that Spielberg's E.T. and Stranger Things both have characters called Mike and Steve.

(60) Finn said his lucky number is seven.

(61) Finn is a fan of Sushi.

(62) Finn is a fan of the vintage pop group Tears for Fears.

(63) Finn said that because Mike in Stranger Things and Richie in Stephen King's IT are very different characters, it was a fun acting challenge to play both roles around the same time.

(64) The children in the cast had to arrange their schooling around Stranger Things and were assigned tutors and a classroom on the set.

(65) Althout set in Indiana, Stranger Things is produced in Atlanta, Georgia.

(66) Finn said he likes shooting Stranger Things in Atlanta for many reasons but especially because they have a great vinyl record store he likes to visit.

(67) Finn said that Barcelona is one of his favourite cities.

(68) Stranger Things was a genuine word of mouth phenomenon. The first season did not have a huge amount of publicity or promotion but positive reviews encouraged viewers to seek it out.

(69) The kids in the cast started a group chat called Stranger Texts.

(70) Season one costume designer Kimberly Adams said that social class was a salient factor in choosing the clothes specific characters would wear. "Will is the youngest in the family. His mom doesn't have a lot of money. He would have had hand-me-downs. I really tried to get, same with his brother as well, just that kind of that odd, ill-fitting, not trendy-of-the-time kind of fit. Different than somebody like Mike, whose family was upper-middle class and conservative. He would have had

newer things for the school year."

(71) The kids in Stranger Things were given relatively little makeup because the Duffers thought it would be more realistic if they had a few spots and blemishes.

(72) Finn said he is an outdoors person and likes to go out and play sports.

(73) Finn as Mike Wheeler has seventy lines in The Weirdo on Maple Street. This is the most lines any character has in any episode of season one of Stranger Things.

(74) The parents and siblings of the children in the Stranger Things cast were a regular presence on the set during season one.

(75) Finn considers himself to be something of a donut connoisseur.

(76) In the Stranger Things season one finale, Eleven is exhausted after dispatching the agents in the corridor and has to be carried by Dustin. In the script it is Mike who carries Eleven but Finn found it too difficult to run and carry Millie Bobby Brown at the same time. Gaten Matarazzo had no such trouble.

(77) Finn was the lead singer for a Vancouver band named Calpurnia from 2017 to 2019. The band released an EP and did several famous covers.

(78) Of the end of his band Calpurnia, Finn said - "Part of the reason why Calpurnia began to become a chore instead of [making] fun music is that we had to tour in order to make the label money. Obviously, that's how they make money, and they need to survive. But I can't always tour because I act, and that is first and foremost and the reason why people give me the opportunities. [Touring] became really hard to do."

(79) Finn is now in a band called The Aubreys which consists of him and his former Calpurnia colleague Malcom Craig. Finn said that because there are less people in The Aubreys this means there are less discussions about everything and so as a consequence the new band takes up less of his time. The Aubreys have released an EP.

(80) Finn said he had no idea that Stranger Things was going to become so popular and successful. "We just thought we were filming this secret thing that no one knew about. Which we were. No one knew what we were doing. Netflix was kind of hands-off. We thought maybe it would become a cult classic, and we'll come back to it in 30 years and be really proud of doing it."

(81) Finn said he nearly quit acting before Stranger Things and Stephen King's IT came along.

(82) Finn said he would like to be a director. In 2020 he directed a Canadian short film called Night Shifts.

(83) Life imitated art in 2019 when Finn Wolfhard was cast in a new Ghostbusters film Ghostbusters: Afterlife. Mike Wheeler is a big Ghostbusters fan in Stranger Things.

(84) At the time of writing, Finn has 41 million followers on Instagram.

(85) Finn deleted his Twitter account in 2020.

(86) Finn feels the character of Mike Wheeler in Stranger Things is quite similar to his real self.

(87) David Harbour (who plays Hopper) said it has been amazing to watch the children grow up so fast in Stranger Things. "One of the most profound things about the show in general, and it's not even acting or writing or anything, is to watch these kids grow up in real time. That's what I'm struck most by, like I remember Finn Wolfhard's little fat face when

[the show began]. And now he's like a big old rock star with chiselled features."

(88) Finn and the main child actors in season one of Stranger Things were alleged to have earned $30,000 an episode. The success of the show meant they would get much more than this in future seasons.

(89) As of 2021, Finn has an estimated net worth of $4 million.

(90) Finn said of his character Mike Wheeler in season one of Stranger Things - "He can be really precocious at times, really funny, and then really serious — solemnly serious about finding his best friend, Will. And I think that's why I like him, because he can be so relatable to people who grew up in the '80s. They can be like, 'Hey, I was kind of like that,' or 'I had a friend like that."

(91) Finn is notoriously private and doesn't share much information about his personal life.

(92) At the time of writing, it is believed that Finn is dating the actress Elsie Richter.

(93) Finn has been the cover model of GQ Korea.

(94) Finn made his debut as a Fashion model on Saint Laurent's Fall/Winter '19 campaign on May 27, 2019.

(95) Finn says that he listens to The Beatles every single day.

(96) Finn said he bases the reactions of Mike Wheeler to how he might react himself in real life.

(97) As he is a proud Canadian himself, Finn must have been happy to hear that Canada was where Stranger Things went viral the quickest.

(98) Mike Wheeler might have a poster for John Carpenter's The Thing in season one of Stranger Things but it's difficult to see how he would know too much of this film. The Thing was not yet on VHS in 1983 and was R-rated in cinemas. Although a revered cult classic today, the movie got terrible reviews when it came out too.

(99) Millie Bobby Brown hated being kissed by Finn in the Stranger Things season one finale. She would enjoy kissing scenes more when she got a bit older.

(100) The Duffers said that the scene in season one of Stranger Things where the kids are fugitives and hide in the abandoned bus became something of an ordeal because one of the boys decided to break wind.

(101) Mike pretends to be sick in season one of Stranger Things so he can blag a day off school and be with Eleven. This appears to be a reference to the cult John Hughes film Ferris Bueller's Day Off - where Matthew Broderick's Ferris pretends to be sick so he can get off school and have a fun day out in Chicago.

(102) The Ghostbusters costumes in Stranger Things 2 were really modified mechanic uniforms.

(103) On wearing eighties fashions in Stranger Things, Finn said - "Oh man, I loved all the '80s clothes that I wear. I mean, the corduroys are pretty tight, but I love Mike's style – it's really cool."

(104) It was Millie Bobby Brown's idea for Mike and Eleven to kiss in the Stranger Things 2 finale.

(105) Finn is a fan of the cult 70s movie Harold & Maude.

(106) Finn does actually play Dungeons & Dragons in real life. He said he acted as the gamesmaster for his former band and also had some D&D sessions to pass the time during the

COVID lockdowns.

(107) Finn had to learn a Russian accent to play Boris Pavlikovsky in the 2019 film The Goldfinch.

(108) Regarding fame and celebrity, Finn said - "A lot of parts are hard about it. But I'm having fun."

(109) Finn loves Air Jordan sneakers.

(110) The Duffers and Shawn Levy had to ask permission from Dan Aykroyd and Ivan Reitman (Aykroyd and Reitman held the rights to Ghostbusters) to put the boys in Ghostbusters costumes for Stranger Things 2. Aykroyd was a fan of Stranger Things so this didn't turn out to be a problem.

(111) Stranger Things 2 saw a notable decrease in dialogue given to Finn as Mike Wheeler. Finn had 199 less lines in season two than in season one. This was a natural consequence of the fact that in season two Mike was not the focus of the plot in the way that he was in season one.

(112) The cast of Stranger Things bonded very quickly on season one. The children, who aside from Gaten Matarazzo and Caleb McLaughlin had never met before, all became close right from the start.

(113) Stranger Things 3 was a tough shoot at times for Finn because he was also shooting IT: Chapter Two at the same time. Finn was exhausted when shooting on both projects was completed.

(114) Despite the stress of fame, Finn said he never pined to be an ordinary run of the mill kid. "The normal teenage experience is you go to school and you go to parties once in a while. I've never really been into that stuff. What I like doing all the time is the stuff I like to do: movies and music."

(115) The children in Stranger Things keep in touch through

TRC-214 Radio Shack walkie-talkies. These are from the 1984 Radio Shack catalogue (a mild anachronism) and somewhat high end for kids to own (these walkie-talkies were more commonly used by employees on large construction sites) but they serve their function in Stranger Things by allowing the children to communicate and simultaneously add another retro eighties veneer to the show.

(116) It was rather ironic that Finn was cast in Stephen King's IT because the Stranger Things creators (the Duffer brothers obviously) had always wanted to make a film adaptation of this themselves.

(117) Despite their obvious similarities, it was a complete coincidence that Finn was cast in Stranger Things and Stephen King's IT around the same time.

(118) Finn said the audition process for Ghostbusters: Afterlife was so secretive he had no idea he was even auditioning for Ghostbusters!

(119) Finn is a fan of the 90s rock band Nirvana.

(120) In 2019, Finn said of Ghostbusters: Afterlife - "Dude, it's one of the most fun sets I've ever been on. Jason Reitman is an amazing director; he's really amazing with his actors and crew. He creates a family relationship on set, so it's been really fun. We'll be done soon, and I think a lot of people are going to love it. I'm really excited. It's genuinely a really beautiful film, and I'm really excited for people to see it. It's really faithful."

(121) Sadly, Ghostbusters: Afterlife was one of but many films delayed by COVID.

(122) Mr Clarke actor Randy Havens said that on season one of Stranger Things it was hard not to fluff takes because the kids always made him laugh.

(123) Finn likes Chinese food.

(124) Despite his fame, Finn says he can suffer from anxiety. "As I suffer anxiety in anticipation, the more experience I have in something, the more it calms me down. With each new set, I'm always nervous at the beginning. I know it's normal, like with the first day of school. But still it is a bit overwhelming. After a few days things improve."

(125) Millie Bobby Brown said Finn and the boys in Stranger Things drove her a bit loopy during the production of season one.

(126) Finn has done a photoshoot for Elle magazine.

(127) Finn is a big Al Pacino fan.

(128) Finn loves skateboarding. He said has been skateboarding since he was seven.

(129) It's probably fair to say that Finn has found it more difficult to adjust to fame than his Stranger Things co-star Millie Bobby Brown. Millie seems to be having the time of her life (for the most part) but you get the impression that it wouldn't especially bother Finn if no one wanted his autograph or picture.

(130) While the Stranger Things props department went to great lengths to make everything authentic and did much research on Dungeons & Dragons, there are some mistakes. The Demogorgon figurine belonging to Mike Wheeler in (the 1983 set) season one only came out in 1984.

(131) Finn's father is involved in aboriginal land claims research.

(132) In the scenes in Stranger Things where the characters are talking on walkie-talkies, the dialogue coming through the walkie-talkies is spoken to the actor on the set so they can react in a natural way.

(133) Finn is a fan of ramen noodles.

(134) Finn said that The Hobbit is one of his favourite books.

(135) When they made season one of Stranger Things, the cast had no idea if there would be a season two.

(136) Finn said he found Stranger Things quite scary when he watched it for the first time. "The first time I saw episode one, my heart was beating watching that beginning scene where the scientist is running down the hallway."

(137) Mike Wheeler has a calculator watch in Stranger Things. These were popular in the 1980s.

(138) When season one of Stranger Things was a big hit in 2016, the kids in the show went out trick or treating for Halloween. They found though that no one deduced who they really were.

(139) Finn collects retro video games. He is a big fan of the Super Nintendo.

(140) Finn attended St. Patrick Regional Secondary School in Vancouver.

(141) Finn graduated from high school in 2020.

(142) Finn is the second youngest of the four main boys in Stranger Things. Noah Schnapp (who plays will Byers) is the youngest.

(143) Finn can play the guitar, drums, and piano.

(144) Finn said Final Fantasy 1 was the first video game he ever played.

(145) Finn is a fan of the 1980s Norwegian pop group A-Ha.

(146) Finn likes burgers and hot dogs.

(147) Charlie Heaton (who plays Jonathan Byers in Stranger Things) said he was amazed at how big Finn and the kids were when they came back to shoot Stranger Things 3. "As for the kids, when Stranger Things began, they were 10 or 11 but they are growing into their adolescence now. They get so much taller, every year I come back. I think Finn is taller than me now. It's crazy watching them all grow up and seeing them all handle the success is incredible. They grow up and they grow up fast."

(149) In the penultimate episode of Stranger Things 2, Mike Wheeler picks up a trophy to brandish as a weapon during the cabin siege. This was a suggestion by Finn Wolfhard because he thought it would be an amusingly bizarre little detail in the scene. A small trophy obviously isn't going to be of any use whatsoever in fending off a frenzied attack by DemoDogs.

(150) In the first episode of Stranger Things 3, Mike and the kids are surreptitiously smuggled into the Starcourt Mall cinema by Steve to watch a horror movie. The movie is then interrupted by a power failure in Hawkins. The film playing is 1985's Day of the Dead. Day of the Dead was the conclusion of George A Romero's famous zombie trilogy and followed on from Night of the Living Dead (1968) and Dawn of the Dead (1978). This series of films was a huge influence on both the comic book and television version of The Walking Dead. The specific scene that plays in the mall cinema before the power failure is the beginning of the movie when the heroine Sarah (Lori Cardelle) is suffering from nightmares and dreams of zombie hands smashing through a wall.

(151) On navigating fame at a young age, Finn said - "I have great parents, a great family, and people who support me, but who also keep me in line. I have been weirdly disciplined since I was seven or eight years old."

(152) Finn loves ice-cream.

(153) Finn's favourite colours are yellow and amber.

(154) Finn is a fan of the Dustin Hoffman film the Graduate.

(155) Finn is a fan of the singer-songwriter Greta Kline.

(156) Finn says that nervousness is an unavoidable part of going on the stage with his band. "You need to have those nerves to get your energy up. In New York I had pretty bad anxiety the day before, but I kind of just got it together near the show. Because I think what really gets me is anticipation. It's just waiting there. Like I've gotta just go do it, you know what I mean?"

(157) Finn is believed to be derived from the Old Norse personal name and byname Finnr.

(158) Finn could also be derived from the Irish Fionn - which means fair.

(159) Finn said he always listens to music in the morning.

(160) Finn said he gets bored very quickly if he has any spare time.

(161) Finn has done some voice acting for Netflix's Carmen Sandiego TV series.

(162) Finn is a fan of the film Attack the Block.

(163) Finn is a fan of the film Leon. This featured a very early role for Natalie Portman.

(164) Stranger Things is scary but not TOO scary. The intention was to be like a PG-13 horror/fantasy film.

(165) Finn is a fan of The Cure. He has this in common with

Stranger Things co-star Charlie Heaton.

(166) The special effects on season one were only completed days before Stranger Things was due to begin streaming on Netflix.

(167) The scene at the end of The Mind Flayer in Stranger Things 2 when Eleven returns and is reunited with Mike feels rather like a homage to the scene in Alien Resurrection where Winona Ryder's android character Call is revealed again despite apparently just dying.

(168) In the first episode of season two of Stranger Things, Mike is sorting out some of his old toys to give away and becomes reflective when he picks up a dinosaur toy. This is because that was the first toy he showed Eleven when she lived in his basement in season one.

(169) Stranger Things producer and director Shawn Levy said that casting children is quite complex.

"I'm looking for not only talent, but that special synchronicity between the actor and the character. So, with the kids on our show, we definitely talk with them more before and after their reading than we do with most adults auditioning. With an adult actor, you're betting so much on the reading. With a kid actor, you're betting just as much on their innate quality in real life in the room. I can tell you for a fact we saw 1,000 kids [for] Stranger Things, and many, many talented kids didn't get the part.

I always tell my actor friends, you can nail an audition and you can be incredibly talented, and sometimes you still won't get the part if it's not in sync with the filmmakers' vision of that character and their feeling—or lack of feeling)—that that person is in the room with them. So much of it comes down to that stuff beyond an actor's control. That's important to remember so you don't beat yourself up for the wrong reasons."

(170) Finn is a big fan of the film Heathers. This movie supplied an early role for Winona Ryder.

(171) Finn said he loves cinnamon buns.

(172) Finn said he likes music concerts to be quite rowdy. He likes everyone moving around and dancing.

(173) Finn is a fan of Billie Eilish.

(174) Finn is a fan of The Clash. The Clash were a British punk rock band who formed in 1976. Their song Should I Stay or Should I Go features heavily in season one of Stranger Things.

(175) Finn is a fan of K-pop group Blackpink.

(176) Finn said of Stranger Things - "It's really cool when the thing you are working on as a small team gets embraced by millions, but in the end, it's about your character and the script and your director and the rest of the cast and crew."

(177) When they were still pitching Montauk (soon to become Stranger Things), the Duffers cut together a concept trailer composed of classic eighties film clips backed with a John Carpenter score. Although there were no scripts when the actors were cast, the actors were all shown the test trailer the Duffers had designed using iconic moments from 1980s fantasy movies. The actors therefore understood what the Duffers were trying to do and were excited about the potential of the concept.

(178) Finn is a fan of the film Close Encounters of the Third Kind.

(179) Finn said he isn't a huge fan of the bike that Mike Wheeler rides in Stranger Things. "They built it with different parts. The weight was all off and the bicycle seat was heavier than the wheels. It was hard to get up hills. You could just get

to a certain speed and just stop. That was really hard to do just to have someone on the back of you at the same time. We've still got a couple years until I get completely sick of it."

(180) Finn said his dad played Dungeons & Dragons when he was a kid so was able to teach him about the game in preparation for playing Mike Wheeler in Stranger Things.

(181) Even though one of his early roles was in the television show Supernatural, Finn said he never watched the show himself.

(182) Finn is a fan of the TV show It's Always Sunny in Philadelphia.

(183) Finn was included in 'Forbes 30 under 30' class of 2020 in the field of acting and entertainment.

(184) Finn said that photography is one of his hobbies.

(185) Finn said that school was always a struggle for him. "I always felt like everyone was going so much faster than I was and I could never catch up to them."

(186) Finn said he is very eager to avoid typecasting as an actor. He wants to do different parts.

(187) Finn said he did a lot of reading during the COVID lockdowns.

(188) The Duffers Brothers said that Mike Wheeler was more of a 'straight man' in the early concept for Stranger Things but Finn's casting made the character funnier.

(189) Ross Duffer said - "Mike was originally a little bit that Mikey from The Goonies, that Sean Astin soft-spoken dreamer type. But Finn has sort of a weird energy, he's fidgety and he talks really fast. So we sort of, you know at the end of the day this isn't how we originally envisioned it but it's actually much

more interesting than we ever could have imagined. So, we went back and we adjusted the voice of Mike and went from there. The kids really did inform these characters. And to us that's something exciting about television that we can sort of adapt as we're going."

(190) Finn doesn't drink tea or coffee. He said he simply drinks water in the morning.

(191) Finn sent a special message to UNICEF Canada's Youth Activism Summit in 2019.

(192) Finn's former band Calpurnia is named after a character in To Kill A Mockingbird.

(193) Finn said he liked making sci-fi short films when he was a kid.

(194) Finn said that when he went back to school after season one of Stranger Things came out he wasn't really treated any differently by the other pupils.

(195) Finn is a fan of The Velvet Underground.

(196) There is a now a Stranger Things Trivial Pursuit with questions all about the 1980s.

(197) The McFarlane Toys Stranger Things Action Figures include the boys in their Ghostbusters costumes.

(198) The town of Jackson, which doubles for Hawkins, has enjoyed a nice financial boost thanks to all the visits by Stranger Things fans.

(199) The Duffers said they originally wanted Stranger Things 2 to pick up exactly where season one ended but had to do a modest time jump in the end because the kids were changing and growing up.

(200) By the time that Stranger Things 2 came out, the glut of Stranger Things merchandise had snowballed into what you might expect of one of the most popular television shows in the world.

You could buy Stranger Things t-shirts, Stranger Things jigsaw puzzles, Stranger Things Dungeons & Dragons, Stranger Things action figures, Stranger Things cardboard cut-outs, eggo waffle purses, a replica of Steve's baseball bat, Stranger Things candles, a Stranger Things Ouija board, and countless other items. Bars and cafes launched Stranger Things cocktails and Stranger Things pizza. There were a number of Stranger Things pop up bars around the world.

Everyone wanted to celebrate the show. Stranger Things was a genuine global phenomenon that appealed to a broad spectrum of people and ages.

(201) Finn said his first music amp was an Orange Crush.

(202) Finn has been vocal about his dismay at the fact you have to be nineteen to get into music venues in Vancouver. "In Vancouver it's very hard for me to see bands because the venues are 19 and over. I've reached out to the attorney general a few times to get the laws changed, but he obviously doesn't care because he hasn't bothered to reply. It makes it even harder for kids to see bands, and it's killing the culture. Worse, the lesson for me is that if you don't vote and you don't drink, you don't count."

(203) Hollywood News wrote of Finn's short film Night Shifts - 'The story plays out within the confines of a convenience store late at night. The shift is going slowly until someone tries to rob the place, but it turns out there's a connection between cashier and criminal, and events take an unexpected turn. At only just shy of four and a half minutes long, there's obviously not a whole lot of story in Night Shifts, but what there is, generates enough interest and intrigue that we'd be keen to see it expanded into something longer. In fact, the whole short

plays like the opening to movie, maybe some kind of teen comedy in vein of Superbad; one thing that Wolfhard's script has nailed, is the humour. From the writing alone, it's easy to see why Muschietti cast him as the funny guy. The dialogue is tightly written, funny, and conveys an impressive multitude of history and information in such a small amount of time.

Visually, Night Shifts demonstrates that Wolfhard has clearly been paying attention to the directors he has worked with as an actor. There's a certain Stranger Things-like sheen to the look of the convenience store, although here it's much more modern with lots of bright lights and steel tones. The camerawork is also considered, with it acting as the driving force in place of actual action. In the opening moments especially, the camera tracks in and pans round in such a way that it frames the images in an almost graphic novel panel fashion. A clever and stylish little short that more than exemplifies that, should his acting work dry up, Finn Wolfhard has a promising career as a director.'

(204) Finn was under the weather when they shot the Snow Ball scenes in Stranger Things 2 but he managed to get through them in the end.

(205) Finn said he would rather talk to a fan for a few minutes than sign an autograph.

(206) Finn was amazed during a press interview for his horror movie The Turning when he discovered that his young co-star Brooklynn Prince had never heard of One Direction. It was a rare case of Finn feeling old!

(207) Finn described his character Richie in IT as the 'trash mouth' kid.

(208) Finn says that, unlike his Stranger Things co-stars, he isn't very good at pranks.

(209) Finn has quite a dry wit.

(210) Finn has joked that his Stranger Things co-stars always seem to know more about what is going to happen in the story than him.

(211) Finn said he likes Vancouver because the pace of life is slower than most big cities.

(212) Finn thinks the film and television industry should give young people more positions of influence.

(213) Finn has a soft spot for musicals.

(214) Finn said he enjoys visiting Spain.

(215) Finn said he sometimes suffers anxiety in interviews.

(216) According to a YouGov America poll, 40% of the general public have heard of Finn Wolfhard.

(217) Finn has now made three horror movies.

(218) Finn has been named by Variety in their young Hollywood Youth Impact Report consecutively since 2017.

(219) Finn said that Charlie Heaton is the biggest corpser on the Stranger Things set in that he gets the giggles during a take.

(220) The production of Stranger Things 4 was a marathon thanks to the pandemic and COVID protocols. The first footage was shot at the start of 2020 but the fans have to wait until 2022 to watch it.

(221) Finn doesn't seem to have what you would call a lavish celebrity lifestyle. He seems very down to earth.

(222) Finn said he was terrified of horror films as a little kid but soon grew to like them.

(223) Unlike other celebrities his age, Finn doesn't seem to wear hats much.

(224) Finn favours indie rock and pop when it comes to music. He has a few mainstream likes though.

(225) Finn said it will be 'bittersweet' when Stranger Things ends and he has to say goodbye to Mike Wheeler.

(226) Finn said he doesn't mind the travel that comes with his job and that he enjoys visiting new places.

(227) It apparently costs over $100,000 to hire Finn for a speaking event.

(228) Finn is a fan of The Godfather movies - the first two in particular.

(229) The Duffers say that Finn and Gaten Matterazzo were the most knowledgeable of the Stranger Things kids when it comes to eighties movies.

(230) Finn has co-directed a music video.

(231) Finn said he loves the green spaces in Vancouver.

(232) Finn is a big fan of the puppet comedy film Team America.

(233) When the movie IT came out, a YouTuber named James Charles tweeted 'Five minutes in and IT is already awful'. Finn tweeted a great response in which he simply asked 'Why are you on your phone in the movie theater?'

(234) Finn said the greatest gift in the world is to have a job you love.

(235) Finn is famously slender and skinny.

(236) Finn seems to like having long hair.

(237) Finn said he enjoys binging TV shows.

(238) Finn has a Gibson guitar.

(239) Finn is a fan of Robert DeNiro.

(240) It apparently costs around $50,000 to book Finn to make an online speech.

(241) Nancy is rather disgusted in season one of Stranger Things when Mike puts syrup on his scrambled eggs. This is not as eccentric as it might sound though. A surprisingly large number of people like syrup on eggs.

(242) Stranger Things was nominated for a 2017 BAFTA in the best international show category.

(243) Finn doesn't seem to have much interest in cooking.

(244) Finn once said you'd have to be a psychopath to want to be famous.

(245) Finn said he wishes he had more time to watch television shows.

(246) Finn became known as Emo Mike on the set of Stranger Things 2 because Mike Wheeler is more grouchy than he was in season one.

(247) The chapter titles at the start of each episode of Stranger Things are to make it feel like you are digesting a Stephen King novel.

(248) After Stranger Things 2 came out, Millie Bobby Brown was asked who should pick to save in the show out of Hopper and Mike Wheeler. She said she'd save Hopper because David

Harbour would be devastated if she didn't pick his character whereas it wouldn't really bother Finn.

(249) A 2016 poll in Time Out named Hawkins from Stranger Things as the fictional place where people would most like to go on vacation. King's Landing and Hogwarts were second and third.

(250) The kids have some Yoo-hoo drinks in Stranger Things 3. Yoo-hoo is a brand of chocolate beverage that was developed by Natale Olivieri in Garfield, New Jersey in 1928.

(251) When it comes to fashion, Finn is a fan of stripes.

(252) Finn is a fan of pizza.

(253) Finn is a fan of Whitney. This is a band from Chicago.

(254) When the kids try and run away from Brenner and the agents in the school corridor in the Stranger Things season one finale, many felt this was a little Easter egg to the teenagers in John Hughes' The Breakfast Club trying to evade their teacher in the school.

(255) Finn is a fan of the film Juno.

(256) Winona Ryder was bewildered on the set of Stranger Things when Finn and the kids started talking about Snapchat. She thought Snapchat was a cafe.

(257) Finn is a fan of the film Rushmore.

(258) The season one finale of Stranger Things apparently created a surge in demand for chocolate pudding.

(259) Finn is a fan of the 1995 film Kids.

(260) Although Millie Bobby Brown was separate from Finn and the boys for most of season two in her scenes as Eleven,

she saw them on the set all the time because they had their school classes together during the production.

(261) The boys' trick or treat haul in Stranger Things 2 appears to include a Mr. Goodbar. Mr. Goodbar is a candy bar containing peanuts and chocolate. It's easy to spot because of the yellow wrapper.

(262) Finn is a fan of the film Terminator 2: Judgment Day.

(263) There is a thematic connection between John Carpenter's movies and Stranger Things because in Carpenter's films the authorities are not to be trusted and usually out to get us.

(264) Finn is a fan of Nirvanna the Band the Show. Nirvanna the Band the Show is a Canadian mockumentary television series based on the web series of the same name.

(265) The Stranger Things title graphic is instantly nostalgic because large typefaces were very popular in the 1980s.

(266) Finn is a fan of Monty Python.

(267) There appear to be some croquet mallets in the Wheeler garage in season one of Stranger Things. This is a reference to The Shining.

(268) Finn is a fan of the film Inglourious Basterds.

(269) Drew Struzan was a huge influence on the Stranger Things poster art. Struzan did the poster art for Back to the Future, Indiana Jones, and Star Wars.

(270) Finn said of Stranger Things - "Every year, it gets amped up. Every year it gets funnier and darker and sadder, and everything."

(271) Michelin star chef Jordi Roca celebrated the release of

Stranger Things 3 by creating some Stranger Things themed ice cream treats.

(272) Finn said he was somewhat dismayed at the early shows by Calpurnia because the audience kept shouting Stranger Things references.

(273) Season three of Stranger Things was given the go ahead by Netflix before season two have even been finished.

(274) The Goonies had been out for about a month when Stranger Things 3 takes place. However, the movie is not playing at the mall cinema in the show.

(275) Finn is a fan of Joe Pesci.

(276) Finn is a fan of Ryan Reynolds.

(277) Finn is a fan of the pop group Weezer. He has appeared in one of their videos.

(278) Finn said of Mike Wheeler - "He's sort of the leader. He just doesn't give up on things. He doesn't give up on his best friend Will. I think he's really cool, but at the same time he keeps to himself and is really socially awkward. The character was always a mix of so many things. He's a mix of me for sure, as well as Sam from Freaks & Geeks and Mikey from The Goonies."

(279) Finn said he is not great with early mornings and usually wakes up about fifteen minutes before a car is due to pick him up.

(280) Mike Wheeler and the boys use the term 'Code Red' on their walkie-talkies to signify an emergency situation in Stranger Things.

(281) Finn said the kiss between Mike and Eleven in the season one finale of Stranger Things wasn't his first kiss

because he kissed a girl when he was in kindergarten.

(282) In a 2017 interview, Monte Christo Magazine noted that the down to earth Finn turned up for their interview with no entourage or assistants and simply had his dad with him.

(283) Finn is a fan of Alex turner. Alex Turner is an English singer.

(284) Stranger Things costume designer Amy Parris said that they have to have multiples of the kids outfits for stunt doubles and stand-ins to use. This makes the task of sourcing period clothes even more complex.

(285) Finn is a fan of Post Animal. This is band that his Stranger Things co-star Joe Keery used to be in.

(286) The nightmares featuring Baldo the clown that Bob Newby speaks of in Stranger Things 2 are another reference to Pennywise from Stephen King's IT.

(287) In 2019, Finn said - "Right now, surviving mostly means sleeping whenever I can and taking advantage of any hours off to have fun, see friends and saying no to a lot of stuff that if I did do I know I would go over the edge."

(288) Stranger Things has earned four Fangoria Chainsaw Awards.

(289) Finn is a fan of The Front Bottoms. The Front Bottoms are an American folk punk band.

(290) Finn said it was somewhat overwhelming when the first season of Stranger Things became such a phenomenon.

(291) Calpurnia made their EP in Chicago.

(292) Finn said that during production of season one of Stranger Things, after he had done his scenes he was allowed

to go back on the set by the Duffers to watch other scenes
being shot so he could pick up some tips about directing.

(293) Finn is a fan of Sing Street. This is an Irish musical film.

(294) Finn said - "I think the whole thing with Stranger Things
is that it was meant to be, like you said, a homage to those
classic films you mentioned and others which are similar.
There are even some tributes and shots that are almost the
same, but all meant with complete respect to the originals."

(295) Stranger Things takes place in Roane County. This
county doesn't really exist in Indiana.

(296) Finn is a fan of The Nude Party. This is a band from
North Carolina.

(297) The boys have orange lights on their bikes in season one
of Stranger Things. This could be seen as a mistake because
bikes did not use orange lights in the early eighties.

(298) Finn said that life on the Stranger Things set is like
being at summer camp.

(299) Finn is a fan of Car Seat Headrest. Car Seat Headrest is
an American indie band.

(300) Finn is a fan of Keanu Reeves.

(301) Of the other boys in Stranger Things, Finn said - "I took
a lot from Caleb because he's a very good dramatic actor, and
Gaten's a good comedic actor because he just goes with it."

(302) Finn said that making a new season of Stranger Things
is sort of like going back to school.

(303) Finn said when when he was six-years old he saw Steven
Spielberg in the street and tried to run after him. "I just started
running up behind him. I had no fear. Plus I had these giant

boots on, so he probably thought somebody was about to kill him. And then the reveal is, he turns around... and it's just me."

(304) The Observer didn't like Finn's horror movie The Turning very much. 'Believe it or not, The Turning began life as a potential Steven Spielberg project, which if the script turned out anything like one we got here, would have been the cinematic equivalent of Jacques Pépin working at an Arby's. (Instead the Saving Private Ryan maestro is listed as an executive producer.) This is a horror movie as processed cheese sauce—not even the most talented of directors could have come up with something unique or personally expressive given the limits of its intentions and subtlety.'

(305) Finn said of the IT movie - "It's scary, but it won't scare you to the point where you have to leave the theater or anything. You're sort of always laughing. It's so close to a comedy, and it's so close to a drama, and it's so close to a romance. So you know, it's not just a horror movie. It's got a lot of layers."

(306) Finn likes the quote by Bo Burnham - 'If you're an entertainer or actor, you're just in the service industry—just way overpaid.'

(307) The endless Stranger Things fan theories that didn't turn out to be true include the theory that Ted Wheeler is a Soviet spy.

(308) Finn said he doesn't like fruit much so rarely eats any.

(309) After Stranger Things was an instant hit in 2016, Finn and some of the cast and crew visited the White House. They discovered that President Obama was a fan of the show.

(310) Finn said he is a Star Wars fan and even likes the prequel trilogy.

(311) There was the very real prospect of a clash of schedules between It and Stranger Things at one point and it was almost certain that Finn's management, in that scenario, would have chosen a Hollywood movie over Stranger Things. At the time no one heard of Stranger Things and had no idea if it would be any good.

(312) The Stranger Things episode The Body takes its title from the Stephen King novella which was adapted into the classic Rob Reiner film Stand By Me. Stand By Me is one of Finn's favourite films.

(313) Finn has Gremlins and Goonies posters in his room at home.

(314) According to babycenter.com, Finn was the 179th most popular name for baby boys in 2021.

(315) You can now buy a Finn Wolfhard duvet cover.

(316) Finn said he cut his chin on a desk around the time they made season one of Stranger Things so this had to be covered up.

(317) Because Finn has long hair it tends to look like a mullet when he has it straightened. This probably explains why he sticks to the curls.

(318) Finn said he likes Vancouver because people don't make such a big deal of him being Mike from Stranger Things as other places. Maybe they are just more used to seeing him around.

(319) Finn is a fan of the film Let the Right One In.

(320) Finn said he had to improve his diction when he started doing voice acting.

(321) Finn said that the Duffers have never tried to hide his

(expanding) height in Stranger Things.

(322) In 2019, Finn said of watching footage from season one of Stranger Things -" The entire thing is like a time capsule, especially season one. I hardly remember doing it — in a good way. It was such a different kind of thing, and I had never done it before. I don't remember acting; I just remember living on set and learning. I only remember the parts where they cut, which is really weird."

(323) Finn said that shooting IT was a bit more intense than the (more PG-13) horror of Stranger Things.

(324) Finn said he enjoys voice acting because recording studios are fairly nice places to be.

(325) The extras in the high school scenes in season one of Stranger Things were put in light pastel shades to project an eighties aura.

(326) The Duffers cited the short lived sitcom/drama Freaks and Geeks as an (unlikely) influence on Stranger Things. Freaks and Geeks is set in a high school in the early eighties. Finn is a fan of this show.

(327) Stranger Things has some similarities to Paper Girls - a comic by Brian K Vaughan that began in 2015. Paper Girls is set in 1988 and is about four girls who live in a small Cleveland town. While out on their morning paper round on bikes, they stumble into a perplexing science fiction mystery that launches them into alternate realities and the past and future.

(328) Finn said he tends to discover new music through talking with friends rather than streaming sites.

(329) The production of a new season of Stranger Things is an increasingly complex and lengthy operation. Even when the actors have filmed their scenes and gone home it still takes months to complete the digital effects.

(330) The Lovecraft story that has the most in common with Stranger things is the 1920 short story From Beyond. The story is told from the first person perspective of an unnamed narrator and details his experiences with a scientist named Crawford Tillinghast. Tillinghast creates an electronic device that emits a resonance wave, which stimulates an affected person's pineal gland, thereby allowing them to perceive planes of existence outside the scope of accepted reality.

(331) The reason why the Duffers decided not to set (what became) Stranger Things in Montauk was a matter of logistics. Shooting the show on the coast would have left the production at the mercy of the elements.

(332) Finn said he loves the monster from the movie Cloverfield.

(333) Although he did the voice for the Carmen Sandiego animation, Finn was too young to be familiar with the video game series that made the character famous.

(334) It is no coincidence that Stranger Things takes place at a time before our modern day digital overload. The eighties seems a much more innocent and carefree time today because the intrusion of news, information, technology, and media was considerably less claustrophobic.

(335) Despite the pandemic, Finn was able to attend a real graduation ceremony when he left high school. It took place in a church.

(336) Finn is a fan of the 80s werewolf film the Howling.

(337) Finn says he likes the idea of playing darker characters in the future.

(338) Finn is a fan of the 1984 punk drama Suburbia.

(339) Fan casting sites have suggested Finn should play Frank N. Furter in a remake of The Rocky Horror Picture Show.

(340) Finn's band The Aubreys featured on the soundtrack to the Turning.

(341) Finn is a fan of Jay Reatard. Jay Reatard was an American musician who died in 2010.

(342) Finn said he would like to direct a horror film one day.

(343) Finn is a fan of the TV show Family Guy.

(344) Finn voiced Pugsley Addams in The Addams Family animated movie.

(345) The self-deprecating Finn isn't convinced that he's very good at voice acting. "It's so funny. I think I'm really bad at voice acting. But people hire me for it, so thank you! It's just really hard for me. It's way harder for me than acting because you can use your face and slur your words. But with voice acting you have to be clear."

(346) The arcade game with cartoon animation in Stranger Things 2 that Mike and boys seem both enchanted and frustrated with in equal measure is called Dragon's Lair. This was an unusual game that came out in 1983. It featured animation by a former Disney animator named Don Bluth and was more of a choose your fate adventure than an arcade game. The player made a choice and then watched the next animation play out to see if they had made the right choice or the wrong choice. Dragon's Lair was popular at first but this type of game didn't catch on. Watching the game's hero hero Dirk the Daring get killed in cartoon animation simply became annoying (and expensive) for players.

(347) The children in Stranger Things liken the Upside Down to the Plane of Shadows. The Plane of Shadows is a dimension that exists alongside our own reality. It is there all the time in

close proximity but elusive.

(348) Adjusted for inflation, the 2017 film IT was the most successful horror film in history at the American box-office.

(349) Regarding the financial success of IT, Finn said - "I didn't really care if it was a big hit or not because I had so much fun, but I was really pleasantly surprised."

(350) Finn said of his character Richie in Stephen King's IT - "On the outside, you just see him as this shell who's doing jokes for his friends, but on the inside he's a hurt guy—no one really pays attention to him at home. I'd never played a role like that, and I can also be funny all the time, which is a great change. Not that Stranger Things wasn't amazing, but I had more creative freedom in It."

(351) Finn said that John Badham on Directing is one of his favourite books.

(352) Finn said it can be quite tricky to be a child actor because of the scrutiny one is under in the public eye. "When you're in the spotlight as a kid, youcan't make a mistake, or else it's public and your career will be over. It's one of those things where you have to be ultra-vigilant about what you say and what you do."

(353) Finn is a fan of Mudhoney. This is an American rock band.

(354) The San Francisco Chronicle wrote of the II movie - 'Finn Wolfhard, so good in a starring role in Stranger Things, is even better here as foul-mouthed, brazen friend Richie.'

(355) Finn said the worst thing about signing an autograph in the street is that you are then deluged by dozens of other people who want one too.

(356) Finn seems to be quite fond of wearing suits.

(357) When asked who the best actor in Stranger Things was, Finn took the diplomatic approach and said they were all great.

(358) Finn said he isn't much of a breakfast person.

(359) Finn is a fan of the 80s horror comedy Critters.

(360) Finn said that the Duffers gave him a crash course in Dungeons & Dragons in preparation for Stranger Things.

(361) Finn loved the fact that Bill Hader played the adult Richie in the IT sequel because he was a fan of Hader.

(362) Finn said he was told to grow his hair long for Stranger Things 4.

(363) Finn is a fan of board games.

(364) Millie Bobby Brown said the Stranger Things kids never talk about dating.

(365) Finn said for the first ever scene in Stranger Things the Duffers put the boys in the Wheeler basement set for hours to shoot the Dungeons & Dragons game that begins the show. This was a shrewd way to make the boys bond quickly.

(366) Finn is honest enough to have conceded that he probably wouldn't have got a record contract if he wasn't famous from Stranger Things.

(367) Finn said it's always an anxious time when a new season of Stranger Things is released. Thankfully though the reviews have always been good so far.

(368) The 2017 IT film wasn't the first time this story had been adapted. There was a 1990 IT television miniseries. The miniseries is best known for Tim Curry's sinister performance

as Pennywise the Clown.

(369) Finn said he has a deadly fear of rats.

(370) Just before Mike and Eleven kiss at the Snow Ball in Stranger Things 2 you can see Finn whisper a warning to Millie Bobby Brown.

(371) Finn said he would open to appearing in a Marvel movie one day.

(372) On securing the part of Mike Wheeler in Stranger Things, Finn said - 'My agent e-mailed me and said, "This part is perfect for you," because I'm obsessed with retro '80s movies. The Goonies is one of my favorite movies, and Sixteen Candles, Raiders of the Lost Ark — all those movies. So I read the script and I immediately fell in love with it. Then I auditioned for it, and they apparently really liked it, so we Skyped. We talked about movies that we liked, and we just talked like we were best friends, and they were like, "Oh, by the way, do you want to come to L.A. to do a screen test?" And then I did the screen test, and they asked me back again, and that was it."

(373) 70% of viewers who watched up to the second episode of Stranger Things finished the first season.

(374) In the initial plan for the second season of Stranger Things 2, Mike and Eleven were not going to see each other again until the finale.

(375) Finn said he became very close to the other kids in the cast of IT and they were friends away from the screen too.

(376) Finn is a fan of Blink-182.

(377) There was a slight battle between Netflix and the Duffers on Stranger Things 2 when it came to swearing. Netflix wanted to do alternative takes of the scenes where the kids swear so

that bad language was very minimal. The kids in the cast hated this idea because they thought scenes were much funnier with a few stray cuss words by their characters. The Duffers also preferred the takes with the odd cuss word so in the end Netflix conceded.

(378) There is a slight goof in the Ghostbusters scenes in Stranger Things 2 when the boys refer to proton packs. This term was only used in 1989's Ghostbusters II.

(379) The boys have orange lights on their bikes in season one of Stranger Things but the light that comes out is white. This is not so much a mistake but simply a technical necessity by the production designers. Orange light obviously didn't work as well.

(380) Finn said he would love to play Kurt Cobain in a biopic.

(381) Finn wore a suit and turtle neck sweater at the Stranger Things 2 premiere.

(382) Finn is a fan of The Pixies.

(383) Emma Watson was once introduced to the kids from Finn's IT movie at an award show and mistakenly presumed they were the Stranger Things kids.

(384) A number of Stranger Things cast members have to wear wigs to depict 1980s hairstyles but Finn isn't among them so far.

(385) Finn said that although he loves the music score of Stranger Things it hasn't been an influence on his own music.

(386) Ghostbusters: Afterlife has appearances by the original Ghostbusters actors.

(387) Fancasting sites have suggested that Finn would make a good Red Robin in a Batman film.

(388) Finn seems to have enjoyed a fairly charmed life as an actor so far. He hasn't had any notable rejections.

(389) Finn (rather self-deprecatingly) said that although he can play several instruments he can't play any of them very well.

(390) Finn and the other boys in Stranger Things play a lot of video games in the downtime between scenes.

(391) Many of the younger cast members in Stranger Things have stage Broadway backgrounds but Finn is not among them.

(392) Netflix floated the possibility of filming seasons two and three of Stranger Things back to back to mitigate the fact that the children (who were, you might plausibly argue, the trump card of the cast in season one) were growing up fast. The Duffer Brothers did not concur with this plan though. They were perfectly relaxed about the fact that the kids would be growing teenagers in new seasons.

(393) Finn says he uses female deodorant because for some reason it just works better for him.

(394) The Duffers had intended to shoot the Stranger Things 2 Snow Ball scenes in one day (the child extras had only been hired for eight hours) but this proved impossible so they had to get everyone back the next day. Even then, it was still a struggle and they only just managed to shoot everything they needed before the second day was through.

(395) Finn said he enjoyed Stranger Things 3 because he was allowed to improvise some of Mike's dialogue in the scenes between Mike and Eleven.

(396) When they shot season one of Stranger Things, the cast were not given all of the scripts and so for much of the

production they had no idea how it would end.

(397) The Palace Arcade in Stranger Things 2 is named after the 20 Grand Palace Arcade in the 1983 Cold War teen fantasy film WarGames.

(398) The Palace Arcade was a renovated laundromat located on 6500 Church Street in Douglasville, Georgia. The local people in Douglasville were said to be disappointed when they learned the arcade was not permanent and only for scenes in Stranger Things 2. It was so authentic they thought it was a real arcade someone had opened.

(399) Finn once said he didn't enjoy high school and couldn't wait for it to end. That said, he did praise his last school when he graduated.

(400) Finn said that - just like Mike Wheeler in Stranger Things - he loves riding a bike.

(401) Finn and the other boys from Stranger Things did a Mowtown song performance on James Corden.

(402) Finn thinks he has a terrible diet sometimes as a consequence of so much travel and thinks he could improve his eating habits.

(403) Mike's line ("Holy s***! What happened to you?") to Dustin at the Snow Ball dance in Stranger Things 2 is the same as a line Finn Wolfhard has as Richie to Ben Hanscom in the film IT.

(404) Jim Hopper and Mike Wheeler are the only 'regular' characters apart from Eleven who appear in The Lost Sister.

(405) Finn is a fan of the TV show Succession.

(406) Finn thought that dressing up as a Ghostbuster in Stranger Things 2 might preclude him from being in

Ghostbusters: Afterlife but - happily - this wasn't the case.

(407) Finn is quite famous for looking fashion chic as he saunters through airports.

(408) Finn is a fan of Game Grumps. This is a 'Let's play' web series about video games.

(409) Finn is a fan of the film Once Upon a Time in Hollywood.

(410) Finn likes chilli.

(411) Finn got some criticism once for not wishing Millie Bobby Brown happy birthday on social media. Finn had to point out that he had already wished her happy birthday through a private text.

(412) Finn is a fan of the Reebok brand.

(413) Finn wanted to be a professional skate-boarder when he was a kid.

(414) Finn thinks that social media, while annoying at times, has its positive aspects. He has worked with people he met through social media.

(415) The theme of Finn's short film Night Shifts is the sometimes fleeting nature of friendship.

(416) Finn believes the key to coping with fame is to be as normal as possible when you go home and to do ordinary things.

(417) Finn said that when production began on the first season of Stranger Things he was so excited to be there he literally didn't stop talking for weeks.

(418) Finn said it was very exciting to see the Stranger Things

sets for the first time.

(419) The scripts on Stranger Things are quite fluid in that the Duffers like to give themselves enough flexibility to change plot points - even during production. This is why the actors in the show never seem to be completely sure what is actually going to happen in any given season.

(420) Finn appears to be making the transition from child actor to young adult actor fairly smoothly. The general rule with child actors as they grow up is to display range without doing anything too adult too fast.

(421) Finn is a fan of Emma Watson. Emma Watson is a child actor who made a good transition from child roles to grown-up roles.

(422) Finn has never had a regular job.

(423) Millie Bobby Brown said that when Finn and the boys got on her nerves shooting the first season of Stranger Things she would seek sanctuary in Winona Ryder's trailer.

(424) Finn said that, despite his youth, he already feels like something of a horror veteran.

(425) Finn's mother Mary worked for the brand Dormouse Design - which designs kids clothes.

(426) Finn said he started to play the bass guitar when he was seven.

(427) Finn said he liked the concept of Stranger Things so much he would happily have played any role in the show.

(428) Finn prefers to listen to albums on vinyl.

(429) Finn is a fan of The Beastie Boys.

(430) The Aubreys, Finn's new band, did a horror themed music video.

(431) Finn said he doesn't really put much thought into fashion and wears what seems comfortable and sort of individual.

(432) In season one of Stranger Things, the school bully Troy calls Mike's gang losers. This is a reference to the loser's club in Stephen King's IT.

(433) Finn thinks that some of the best music venues are in London.

(434) Finn said he stays with some of his IT co-stars when he's in Los Angeles.

(435) Finn still lives in Vancouver. He hasn't moved to Hollywood yet.

(436) Finn said he loves the hotels in New York.

(437) The Mind Flayer takes on a spider like form in Stranger Things 3 in what it is an obvious homage to Stephen King's IT.

(438) At the premiere party for Stranger Things 2, a number of special Stranger Things drinks were served. These included Pumpkin Ale and UpCider Down.

(439) Mike tries to contact Eleven at 7:40 p.m in Stranger Things 2. 7 + 4 = 11.

(440) Finn said he wouldn't mind being in a Star Wars movie one day.

(441) Finn said he isn't a fan of men's cologne and strong smelling beauty products.

(442) Finn said he likes to collect blu-ray movies.

(443) At the school memorial for Will Byers in season one of Stranger Things, Mike Wheeler refers to those who didn't know Will (but are now pretending to care) as phonies. This appears to be a reference to Holden Caulfield in The Catcher in the Rye.

(444) No one was more delighted by the success of Stranger Things than the Kellogg Company. The new interest in Eggo waffles through Stranger Things saw a noticeable spike in Kellogg's stock price on the financial markets.

(445) There is a Family Feud board game in the Wheeler basement in Stranger Things 2.

(446) A Stranger Things Edition Polaroid Camera was released in 2019. It was priced at $99.

(447) Number crunching by Parrot Analytics suggested that Stranger Things 3 recorded over three times the viewer demand of Game of Thrones.

(448) The Toronto Star wrote of the IT movie - 'The young actors pull off the unlikely feat of stealing It from It. As Bill's best friend Richie, Vancouver actor Finn Wolfhard is charming in what could have been just another nerd role, proving his breakout performance on Stranger Things was more than beginner's luck.'

(449) Finn has joked that he'll probably get fat when his metabolism slows down.

(450) Finn is a fan of Ryan Gosling.

(451) Finn doesn't seem to have many brand contracts or endorsements compared to Millie Bobby Brown.

(452) Finn often seems to joke that actors aren't very bright.

(453) Finn said that when he became famous his family had to change their telephone number.

(454) The Duffers say that they don't mind the fact that the children in Stranger Things are obviously older and more grown-up in each new season.

"It forces the show to evolve and change, because the kids are changing. Even if we wanted it to be static and we wanted to continually recycle the same storyline — and we don't — we would be unable to, just because the kids are changing. It's cool, though. The audience is going to be able to watch these kids come of age every year. The closest example is Harry Potter. Watching those kids and actors grow up in front of the camera was, to me, very powerful."

(455) Finn said - "I never liked horror up until I was like 10 years old. A lot of it is coincidence that I've done [so much] horror. But I love horror because what makes a great horror movie is that it's not just scary, it's [a little of] everything. In a real-life horrifying situation there's always [some] comedy or something sad. I think that's in all the horror stuff I've done because I try to make it the realest [portrayal]."

(456) Northern Trannsmissions wrote of Calpurnia's album Scout - 'For a bunch of young Canadians, Calpurnia prove age and fame aren't a factor in what makes you a good musician. Using some familiar indie hooks and sounds, the band constantly subvert expectations and play around with their writing. Though it can feel like a blend of ideas you've heard before, the way Calpurnia blends all their influences is what sets them apart. Finn Wolfhard and crew make sure that by the end of the record, you'll want to dance and sing along on your next listen.'

(457) Finn said he couldn't live without his PS4 because he uses it to play video games and watch movies.

(458) Finn failed his driving test twice.

(459) Finn is a fan of the New Zealand band The Clean.

(460) Mike Wheeler has 273 lines in Stranger Things 3. This ranks him fourth when it comes to characters with the most lines after Hopper, Dustin, and Steve.

(461) When Mike Wheeler shouts "It's a trap!" in Stranger Things 2, he is quoting Admiral Ackbar in Return of the Jedi.

(462) When they shot the school classroom Demogorgon showdown in the Stranger Things season one finale, the children had the giggles and kept laughing.

(463) Finn is a fan of Brad Pitt.

(464) Finn is a fan of the singer Elliot Smith.

(465) Finn is a fan of Emma Stone.

(466) Eleven uses the static of her television to try and contact Mike in Stranger Things 2. The television set was used as an inanimate source of foreboding and supernatural dread in the film Poltergeist.

(467) Finn is a big fan of the film director Wes Anderson.

(468) The set decorators on season one of Stranger Things trawled through dozens of thrift stores and garage sales to look for items that might be authentic to the middle America of 1983.

(469) Finn says that people say he looks like a young Bob Dylan.

(470) Finn is a big fan of the Netflix show Barry.

(471) Finn said of the Duffer Brothers - "They're amazing, they're like my big brothers. We always had this inside joke

where they basically cast themselves as Mike. He's basically an amalgam of both of them. But it was incredible, they were like big kids but they knew exactly what they wanted."

(472) When it comes to fashion, Finn is a fan of plaid.

(473) A comic called Stranger Things - Zombie Boys has the boys making a horror movie for Halloween. The comic is set between seasons one and two.

(474) Millie Bobby Brown said she was dismayed when she saw that Mike and Eleven were going to break up in Stranger Things 3.

(475) Finn is a big fan of movie soundtracks.

(476) Finn thinks that Vancouver is a good place for artists and creative people to live.

(477) Finn had to do some wire harness work for the scene in season one of Stranger Things where Mike jumps off the quarry ledge.

(478) Natalia Dyer (who plays Nancy Wheeler) said she worries about the fame the younger cast members in Stranger Things had to cope with but thinks they have handled it well.

(479) The real challenge for Finn as an actor will come when he ages out of teen roles.

(480) Finn is a fan of David Bowie.

(481) Finn doesn't seem to be one of those actors who takes themselves too seriously.

(482) Finn fired his first agent after allegations of misconduct were made by some women.

(483) Finn has become a more popular name in recent years

but this trend began before Finn was famous so he can't really take the credit.

(484) Finn is a big fan of comic books.

(485) Millie Bobby Brown had never seen a record player until she visited the Stranger Things sets. This was not the case with Finn though. His parents had a record player.

(486) At the Palace Arcade in Stranger Things 2 you can see a game called Quest for the Space Knife. This game is fictitious and based on the fact that one of the production crew had a music band called Space Knife.

(487) The bicycle chase scene in season one of Stranger Things reveals that Hawkins has an Elm Street.

(488) Finn seems to have the utmost confidence that Ghostbusters: Afterlife is really good.

(489) There have been a number of Stranger Things comics. These comics tend to be prequels or 'side stories' so that they don't clash with the actual TV show.

(490) Finn had some purple tints put in his hair to celebrate the end of shooting on Stranger Things 3.

(491) A deal with Netflix to make Stranger Things only took 24 hours.

(492) Because so many bikes were needed (each of the stunt doubles for the children also had to have a bike) in season one of Stranger Things, the bikes in the show are hybrids of different parts (mostly BMX) to create the appearance of early 80s bikes.

(493) The swoosh of the titles at the end of the Stranger Things title sequence was inspired by the film Bullit.

(494) Finn thinks he eats too much candy.

(495) Noah Schnapp and Gaten Matterazzo both auditioned for the part of Mike Wheeler before being assigned other roles in Stranger Things.

(496) Finn thinks you have to be a bit odd to be entirely comfortable with fame because it isn't a natural state of affairs.

(497) Because he keeps failing his driving test, Finn said he has to get his friends to ferry him around in their cars.

(498) Finn said he keeps in touch with the kids from the IT film and they talk all the time.

(499) Finn said he has a large collection of guitars.

(500) There were whispers before Stranger Things 3 that Mike Wheeler was going to be killed off because Finn was too busy to be in the show anyway. This turned out to be nonsense.

(501) Finn and his parents once got trapped at JFK airport during a snowstorm and had to sleep on the floor.

(502) Finn said that when he went to Barcelona a few years ago he was there for four days before anyone recognised him. He said it was heaven to be anonymous.

(503) Finn has played Dungeons & Dragons online with some of the other Stranger Things cast members.

(504) The popularity of Stranger Things took everyone by surprise. As a consequence of this, it was a difficult adjustment for Finn to deal with overnight fame.

(505) Finn likes the city of Seattle.

(506) Finn said that one of his most memorable trips was when he went to Iceland.

(507) Finn thinks that Mike Wheeler is a trifle more serious than he is in real life.

(508) Finn thinks that appearing in music videos for PUP was his pathway to becoming an actor.

(509) Finn said that The Sauna Battle was the most exhausting episode of Stranger Things to shoot.

(510) Finn said that although he loves music his acting career means that music has never become a priority.

(511) Finn says that Jaws is one of his favourite films.

(512) Finn said he would love to go back the 1980s and watch movies like The Goonies in the cinema.

(513) Finn is a fan of the film director Martin Scorsese.

(514) Millie Bobby Brown said that Finn and the boys spend most of their time talking about video games on the set of Stranger Things.

(515) Joe Keery, who plays Steve Harrington, said the kids in Stranger Things made him a better actor because they are all so good.

(516) Shawn Levy, a producer and director on Stranger Things, said that work is the best decompression chamber for the kids when it comes to dealing with fame.

(517) Finn said he thought his name was strange when he was a kid but he loves it now.

(518) Finn said that Mike Wheeler will always be the part dearest to his heart because it was his big break and launched his career.

(519) Finn said that being an actor is the best film school you could hope for because you learn so much on the set.

(520) Finn said he definitely has a stage persona when it comes to music because he's more shy and retiring in real life.

(521) Finn has watched all of the films The Beatles made.

(522) According to statistics, Finn is second only to Millie Bobby Brown in the Stranger Things cast when it comes to online interest and followers.

(523) Finn said if he became a director he would like to make indie style movies.

(524) Joe Keery, like Finn, has also juggled Stranger Things with being in bands.

(525) Finn said he has a 'crazy energy'.

(526) The Upside Down in Stranger Things was called the Nether in the original scripts.

(527) The first season of Stranger Things required around 150 wigs for the cast and extras.

(528) Mike Wheeler has a poster for Jim Henson's eighties fantasy film The Dark Crystal on his wall in season one of Stranger Things.

(529) Finn said that after Stranger Things 2 came out he got asked to attend a lot of school dances. He declined these invitations.

(530) Finn is apparently not a huge fan of TikTok.

(531) Finn has been on the cover of GQ Spain.

(532) Finn said - "I think Stranger Things might be the

number one reason why this nostalgia thing has kicked in. But I think why I love Stranger Things is that it's not just nostalgia. You have some of these things come out and just be copycats of Stranger Things and kind of only take the nostalgia out of it. What's great about Stranger Things is that it's not just about the '80s. Yeah, that's the time it's set in, but it's about these characters and the situations that they're in, and not the time. I think it's definitely interesting and weird."

(533) It took a week to shoot the scenes in the Stranger Things 3 episode The Sauna Test where the kids trap Billy in the sauna.

(534) Finn said it was the written part of the driving test that he keeps failing and has problems with.

(535) Finn competed against Noah Schnapp, Gaten Matarazzo, and Caleb McLaughlin in a 2017 episode of Spike's Lip Sync Battle.

(536) Finn is with the talent agency CAA.

(537) Finn appeared in the 2020 anthology comedy Omniboat: A Fast Boat Fantasia.

(538) In 2020 Finn appeared in the short film Rules for Werewolves. This is set to be expanded into a full feature.

(539) In 2020, Finn appeared in Home Movie: The Princess Bride. This was a Jason Reitman web series to raise money for charity during the COVID lockdowns.

(540) Finn is a voice actor in the forthcoming Guillermo del Toro animated version of Pinocchio.

(541) Finn is a fan of Joaquin Phoenix.

(542) Finn is a fan of the band Green Day.

(543) Finn is a fan of Amy Adams.

(544) You can see a 1984 election sign for President Reagan outside the Wheeler house in Stranger Things 2. Dustin's mother is supporting Walter Mondale.

(545) Finn is a fan of the dark anthology television show Black Mirror.

(546) Netflix were very 'hands off' when Stranger Things went into production. This gave the Duffer Brothers creative freedom - which was obviously an advantage to the show.

(547) In 2017, Finn took to social media to complain about online harassment of him and his fellow Stranger Things cast members. "Hey everybody! I don't wanna ex-communicate anyone from this fandom, but if you are for real you will not harass my friends, or co-workers. Ya'll know who you are. Why I even have to tweet that, I don't know. Anyone who calls themselves a 'fan' and actively goes after someone for literally acting and doing their job is ridiculous. Think b4 ya type boiiii."

(548) In 2019, Stranger Things actors Finn and Sadie Sink partnered with Pull&Bear for a new capsule collection inspired by Californian style for the summer.

(549) You can now buy Finn Wolfhard mugs and stickers.

(550) A Richie Tozier Funko Pop with Finn's autograph on the box can sell for over $300.

(551) Finn describes his fashion as a mix of skater fashion and seventies rock.

(552) When Cary Fukunaga departed from IT as the director, Finn thought he would lose the part of Richie because he presumed he'd probably be too old by the time they got a new director and started production. Thankfully though this didn't

transpire in the end.

(553) Finn is a fan of the film Pan's Labyrinth.

(554) Finn doesn't believe you need any formal training to be an actor. He said it's best to just jump in and do it.

(555) Finn loves Harry Potter and has done a marathon of all the movies.

(556) When Finn did a quiz to see which Stranger Things character he was most like he ended up as Will Byers.

(557) The Upside Down was not supposed to feature much in the original plans for Stranger Things. It was supposed to be a place that was largely unseen and would have to be imagined by the audience.

(558) Finn is a fan of Judd Apatow.

(559) Finn said the first album he purchased with his own money was The Suburbs by Arcade Fire.

(560) Finn is a fan of the rock band Modern Baseball. Modern Baseball broke up in 2016.

(561) Finn said he doesn't mind a bit of karaoke.

(562) A survey in 2017 found 31% of young adults had watched all the episodes of Stranger Things.

(563) Finn is a fan of Members Only jackets from the 1980s.

(564) Finn said that Help! is his favourite Beatles album.

(565) Finn is a fan of Julianne Moore.

(566) Finn said the first concert he went to was Coldplay at Rogers Arena in Vancouver.

(567) The kids in the Stranger things cast all had stunt doubles for some of the bike scenes.

(568) The name the boys in season one of Stranger Things give their mission to find Will Byers is Operation Mirkwood. Mirkwood was a great forest in Middle-earth in the books of Tolkien.

(569) A piece of Stranger Things art with Finn's signature usually sells for around $70.

(570) The sequence in the Stranger Things 3 episode The Spy where the soldiers entered the tunnels and are wiped out obviously owes much to the Colonial Marines coming off second best when they investigate the Xenomorph tunnels of the colony in James Cameron's Aliens.

(571) Finn is a fan of Jonah Hill.

(572) Finn has used merchandise to raise money for children of indigenous communities.

(573) In 2020, Finn was a voice actor in the Adult Swim animated special Smiling Friends. Finn's brother Nick was also involved in this project.

(574) Stranger Things 2 began production with a secret codename in an attempt to avoid media attention and potential spoilers.

(575) Stranger Things 3 took eight months to shoot.

(576) At the start of Stranger Things 2, we see Mike and the boys playing Dragon's Lair in the Palace Arcade. What we see though is not the actual game playing but merely animation that was used in advance commercials for the arcade machine.

(577) The Mind Flayer in Stranger Things 2 seems to be

inspired by Louise Bourgeois' spider like sculpture Maman.

(578) In the hospital scenes in Stranger Things 3, the medical uniforms and logos are the same as those in the 1981 horror sequel Halloween II. This is a nice little Easter egg for horror fans.

(579) Finn said he has watched all the John Hughes movies. Hughes was known for 80s teen dramas like The Breakfast Club and Pretty in Pink.

(580) Finn said that his favourite Nirvana album is Bleach.

(581) After Finn and Millie Bobby Brown kissed at the Snow Ball in the Stranger Things 2 finale, the extras gave them a round of applause.

(582) One of the keys to the success of Stranger Things is that it appeals to people of all ages.

(583) Over 360,000 people binged Stranger Things 2 inside a day when it was released.

(584) One sequence the Duffers were unsatisfied with in season one of Stranger Things but couldn't change was the scene where Mike jumps off the quarry ledge (because Troy is threatening Dustin with a knife and has ordered Mike to jump) and is then levitated back to safe ground by the returning Eleven. The Duffers thought it looked too fake when Mike is levitated back up through the air but there simply wasn't sufficient time or money to do this sequence all over again from scratch.

(585) When Will tells Joyce he isn't frightened of horror movies in season one of Stranger Things, she replies "Oh yeah? Not even of... clowns?" This is obviously a reference to Pennywise from Stephen King's IT.

(586) Finn is a fan of Levi pants.

(587) Finn said - "My parents were in high school and college in the '80s, so let's just say I've heard some stuff, man. We listen to a lot of music and watch lots of great films, but the real context they provide from that era is about politics."

(588) Finn said he isn't very fashionable at home and tends to lounge around in sweatpants.

(589) Finn is a fan of animated films.

(590) Finn said of the original 1990 television miniseries adaptation of Stephen King's IT - "A lot of people grew up with the original movie and it was terrifying for them. I talked with the Duffer Brothers about it and when they were kids they were terrified of it. It was this B movie miniseries, pretty groundbreaking for its time, but if you watch it now it's just so campy. So the new one is trying to make it better. It's super dark and really serious. I think it's the perfect homage to the book."

(591) Finn said of the relationship between Mike and Eleven in season one of Stranger Things - "It's one of those things where it's sort of timid and weird, but he really cares for her. He feels like he's protecting her from these terrible people and this outside world. She doesn't know what's happening and Mike doesn't know what's happening, but it's all really complicated. But yeah, it's definitely like a young love sort of situation."

(592) Finn said he enjoyed visiting the guitar shops in Japan.

(593) Finn said he took a lot of walks when COVID shut everything down and he couldn't go out and work.

(594) When the second season of Stranger Things became available on Netflix, fifteen million viewers streamed the new season inside three days.

(595) Given the prevalence of Broadway kids and would be

singers and musicians in the cast, there is apparently a lot of singing on the set of Stranger Things.

(596) Finn has more than one Fender guitar.

(597) David Harbour, to get into character as the grouchy and lonely Hopper in Stranger Things, attempted some method acting and tried to keep his distance from the children in the cast at first. This didn't last though and he soon became one of the gang on the set.

(598) Finn said one of his most memorable trips was to the Aztec pyramids at Teotihuacan in Mexico.

(599) Finn has joked that he's a bit gangly and awkward.

(600) The Duffer Brothers said that Finn's language got a bit saltier when he came back from shooting IT as a consequence of playing the foul-mouthed Richie.

(601) The extras at the Snow Ball dance for Stranger Things 2 were told they were appearing in a show called Wonder View in order to maintain secrecy.

(602) Millie Bobby Brown said that in real life Finn is a very laid-back and relaxed person.

(603) Netflix began in 1997. In the early days of the company they were a DVD rental business. They began producing their own content in 2013.

(604) Research in 2019 found that 14% of former Netflix members planned to buy a new subscription so they could watch Stranger Things 3.

(605) Finn is estimated to have made around a million dollars from his music career.

(606) The arcade machines in Stranger Things 2 were not

authentic to 1984 because they have modern flat screens.

(607) Finn said - "What's frustrating is how much social media drives creative choice. Actors should be able to just act, but instead they have to worry about posting and how many followers they have. I am glad that people follow me and like my posts, but I'm not hiring bot farms to boost the numbers and I'm not changing who I am or what I believe in or how I post because I'm doing this project now or that project next week."

(608) Finn is a fan King Gizzard and the Lizard Wizard. This is an Australian rock band.

(609) Finn is a fan of Thrasher hoodies.

(610) The Wheeler family in Stranger Things seem quite fond of tater tots. Tater tots are grated potatoes formed into small cylinders and deep-fried, often served as a side dish. The name "tater tot" is a registered trademark of the American frozen food company Ore-Ida.

(611) The Duffer Brothers wrote a thirty page document that established the ground rules for the Upside Down in Stranger Things. This enabled the set designers and special effects team to have a clearer idea of what was expected of them. The document did not though explain what the Upside Down was. The Duffers thought the Upside Down would be much scarier if it retained some mystery and we didn't truly understand it.

(612) Finn says he plays Call of Duty multiplayer with friends.

(613) Finn is a fan of the Sonic video games.

(614) Finn is a big fan of Tokyo.

(615) Finn says the Xenomorph in Alien is one of his favourite movie monsters.

(616) When it comes to being famous, Finn once said - "Some things just aren't cool. Like, a person came up to me on a train just because she'd seen someone take a picture of me."

(617) Finn said he was quite touched when some Stranger Things fans made a giant quilt with Mike Wheeler's face on it.

(618) The Stingray Blog wrote of Calpurnia's album Scout - 'The quartet has brought us something that no other band today can come close to equalling – pure indie-rock/new wave. Unlike the many bands that use each new EP release as a way of experimenting and finding their sound but failing miserably, Calpurnia sounds more accomplished than ever. Scout brings with it a relaxed atmosphere coupled with splashes of color and the cheeky bounce of indie-rock. Listening from start to finish, you can get lost in the static, only to suddenly open your eyes and be surprised as to where you've ended up. This record gives us hope for the future. These kids have made it very clear that they won't stop exploring.'

(619) In season three of Stranger Things, Eleven has a photo by her bed of Mike in his Ghostbusters uniform.

(620) Season one was so popular that Stranger Things was the top streamed showed of 2016 in many countries around the world. These included Japan, Australia, and Germany.

(621) When the boys and Eleven walk the train tracks in the woods during season one of Stranger Things this is an obvious reference to the film Stand By Me.

(622) The casting department on Stranger Things looked at nearly a thousand boys when they were casting the roles of Dustin, Mike, Lucas, and Will for season one.

(623) Finn has been on vacation in Hawaii.

(624) Before Stranger things came along, Finn was in two little

known indie movies called Aftermath and The Resurrection.

(625) The early version of Dustin's pet Dart (before he started growing) in Stranger Things 2 was depicted by a rubber model on the set. The rubber model of Dart was nicknamed Sushi by the kids.

(626) Finn said it was easy to bond with the other kids in the movie of Stephen King's IT. "It was really odd because we all got along almost immediately. I'd met some of them in the chemistry reads before, but production gave us two weeks to hang out with each other before the movie started. It definitely worked. We did exercises with the acting coach, like putting on heavy 80s rock to stretch and getting into it and then we'd do trust falls where we have to walk around a room and have normal conversations, and once someone says "drop" you have to drop into your partner's arms and they have to get there like no matter what. We'd also go to Wyatt's [Oleff] house—who plays Stanley—for dinner or sleepovers."

(627) Dungeons & Dragons was heavily influenced by Tolkien. Dungeons & Dragons was even subject to legal action from the Tolkien estate for its similarities to Lord of the Rings and The Hobbit.

(628) Finn said that on Stranger Things the cast only get the scripts a few weeks before shooting begins and even then they don't get all of the scripts.

(629) One of the things people find appealing about Stranger Things and the 1980s from a modern vantage point is that it depicts a time when our lives were not completely dominated by technology in the way that they are today.

(630) The sequence that gave the designers and special effects team the most headaches on season one of Stranger Things was the school classroom showdown between Eleven and the Demogorgon in the finale. The lighting and cloud of dust that envelops Eleven and the monster was exceptionally difficult to

get right.

(631) Finn said he watches a lot of YouTube videos.

(632) The 2017 IT movie got pretty good reviews when it came out. The Guardian wrote - 'Flitting between crooked nursery crime chimes and lush orchestral themes, composer Benjamin Wallfisch creates an emotionally resonant score to accompany Muschietti's blend of scares and sentimentality. The result is an energetic romp with crowd-pleasing appeal that isn't afraid to bare its gory teeth. While it may not be as frightening as some hardened horror fans desire, the archetypal terrors and fundamental friendships of King's source are slickly transferred to the screen with a ghoulish enthusiasm that proves hard to resist.'

(633) You can now buy a Finn Wolfhard Lifesize and Mini Cardboard Cutout.

(634) Finn said that success for him is doing what he loves.

(635) Finn is a fan of Leonardo DiCaprio.

(636) Finn says that music has been a good outlet and distraction for coping with the fame of being a well known actor.

(637) When the teenagers are trapped in the Gap store in the finale of Stranger Things 3, there are camera shots which homage Steven Spielberg's The War of the Worlds.

(638) Finn is a fan of the vintage horror film Sleepaway Camp.

(639) Finn is a big fan of the film director Edgar Wright.

(640) Netflix was founded by by Reed Hastings and Marc Randolph in 1997 as a video rental company. Netflix only started producing their own content in 2013.

(641) Finn is a fan of the 1994 film Clerks.

(642) Finn said of making IT - "It was probably one of the best experiences of my life. It was three to four months in Toronto with a bunch of kids I didn't know. And then we became best friends all in a week and then spent every day and every waking hour with each other. It's a bunch of crazy 13-year-olds on set together. We are all best friends. It sounds like a nightmare when I explain it because you don't want to see a bunch of 13-year-olds running around. It was the best and they are still my best friends."

(643) Finn is fan of Scarlett Johansson.

(644) Finn said of the 1980s - "There's something about the independence of it. Like kids could just go off on their bikes and just be home later, you know. There [were] no cellphones so you could get lost and have an adventure without having your parents go crazy and worry for a while."

(645) Finn said of Calpurnia signing with an indie label - "If I was just doing this by myself as the Stranger Things kid, maybe I could have gone to a big label, but I think what I like about indie labels is that they're small, compact and people know what they're doing. The people who started them usually know what young people are listening to and what young people want. It's a real family, they're always at our shows."

(646) Finn says he watches a lot of sketch comedy on YouTube.

(647) The Duffers said it was very deliberate in season one of Stranger Things the way that the different age groups of characters seem to be in different sorts of movies. "For the teens they're more in a classic horror film; John Carpenter's stuff like Halloween or Wes Craven's Nightmare on Elm Street. That's where the teens live. For the kids it's more the adventure thing, like The Goonies or Stand by Me. And then the adults are a bit more in the classic Spielberg movies like

Close Encounters where they're slowly coming to realise that something extraordinary is happening around them and the sense of wonder that provokes. So that was what we were trying to do. Those are some of the big touchstones for us."

(648) Finn said his family have always had dogs and cats.

(649) Season one of Stranger Things takes place in a world of cassette tapes, wall phones, chintz, pastels, Polaroid cameras, digital watches, woodchip, and cathode ray televisions where anything over 20 inches is considered a status symbol.

(650) Finn said he loves hanging around the swimming pool in the summer.

(651) Finn has done some stage diving in his music career.

(652) The first ever concert for Finn's The Turning co-star Brooklynn Prince was to watch Finn's band.

(653) Because of his busy schedule, Finn had to do his voice acting for Carmen Sandiego separate from the other voice actors.

(654) Finn has joked that he should start paying his friends because they are always driving him around after he failed his driving test.

(655) Finn is a fan of the late singer Daniel Johnston.

(656) Finn said Waiting on a Friend by The Rolling Stones is his favourite song.

(657) Kimberly Adams was the costume designer on season one of Stranger Things. The fashion department scoured catalogues and school photo archives from the era to get an idea of what your average person was wearing in 1983. They of course also watched early eighties movies and television.

(658) Finn plays Fortnite.

(659) Finn doesn't have any tattoos.

(660) Finn is a fan of soccer.

(661) Finn said that he and Millie Bobby Brown have no preparation or discussions for kissing scenes in Stranger Things.

(662) Finn is sometimes alleged to have a real crush on Millie Bobby Brown but there's no real way of knowing if this is true or just idle speculation.

(663) Finn said of acting in horror - "When I'm filming, I'm only scared in the moment, while I am actually acting, and not before or after."

(664) Finn said he likes green shirts when it comes to fashion.

(665) Finn said of Paul McCartney - "I love that Paul is still out there, jamming all over the world for us, when he could just be sitting on a beach. The whole experience is so incredibly inspiring."

(666) The Duffer Brothers estimate that they had around fifteen rejections before signing a deal with Netflix to make Stranger Things.

(667) A 1993 X-Files episode called Eve is often alleged to have been an influence on Stranger Things. The story has Mulder and Scully discovering a secret government project that involves children. The children are numbered - with the main kids for the episode named Eve 9 and Eve 10.

(668) The only problem they encountered with Atlanta as a production base for Stranger Things was shooting the Christmas scenes near the end of season one where it is supposed to be cold and frosty. Ice had to be imported in to

make these scenes more authentic.

(669) The Duffers were always adamant throughout the planning and writing that Stranger Things would have a very limited number of episodes. They didn't want their show to ever feel like it was treading water or spreading its premise out too thinly.

(670) Finn said he uses the smiley face the most when it comes to emojis.

(671) Finn has a Rickenbacker 360 guitar.

(672) Asked what his favourite scene in IT was, Finn (jokingly) said - "I like the scene where Eddy falls through the floor and breaks his arm. Because I am a sadist."

(673) Finn is a fan of the cult 1971 British film Melody.

(674) The first teaser trailer for Stranger Things 2 used a real 80s Eggo commercial featuring child actor Jason Hervey. Hervey later became well known for his role as Wayne Arnold in the comedy drama series The Wonder Years.

(675) Finn and the boys said they got fed up wearing shorts in Stranger Things 3. They had to though because that season was set in the summer.

(676) Finn is a fan of volleyball.

(677) The Duffers may have taken some inspiration for Stranger Things from the cult film Donnie Darko. In that movie the teenagers consult their teacher about portals and time travel.

(678) Finn said that bands from the 1960s were the biggest influence on his own music.

(679) Finn is a fan of the TV show American Vandal.

(680) Finn's Stranger Things character Mike Wheeler was born in 1971.

(681) Finn is a fan of the film Babyteeth.

(682) Finn is planning to direct his first full length film. He says it will be a horror comedy set at a summer camp.

(683) Finn is a fan of the American singer Clairo.

(684) Bradley's Big Buy grocery store in Palmetto, Ga (where Eleven steals the waffles in season one of Stranger Things) reported that their sales of Eggo waffles trebled when season three of Stranger Things came out.

(685) When he first became famous Finn was sometimes asked about dating. He would reply that he was still a kid and didn't have that type of personal life.

(686) Stephen King was a big fan of the 2017 adaptation of his IT novel.

(687) David Harbour believes that people like Stranger Things because it depicts a much simpler time. He's obviously not the first person to make this observation. "Nowadays, everything's recorded and everything's documented and they can go look at your Facebook page or your Instagram page. And back then it was like you could really get lost. You and your friends could get lost in the woods and do weird stuff that nobody knew about. And I think there's a sense of that in the show — kids really were able to be kids. Now, I think you have to be savvy. Even as a child, you have to understand the fact that you're being recorded. I think that's part of the larger nostalgia [surrounding the show] is this idea that we're not being so watched."

(688) The product visibility in Stranger Things 3 was valued at $15 million. There is no actual product placement though and

no company paid any money to be in the show.

(689) Chester Rushing, who played Tommy in the first two seasons of Stranger Things, said there was a palpable electricity at the first ever Stranger Things cast reading.

(690) Finn loved the fact that the other characters thought Dustin's girlfriend in Stranger Things 3 was fictitious but she turned out to be real.

(691) The cabin siege is a staple of Stranger Things. This is a common trope in movies from vintage westerns through to films like Straw Dogs and The Evil Dead.

(692) The credits in the Stranger Things opening title sequence are designed to look like a puzzle that is slowly coming together.

(693) Finn said - "Obviously Stranger Things has given me the launching pad to have creative license for whatever I want, and I love doing the show, but when it comes to music, I want to distance myself as much as possible. It would be weird to play a Stranger Things prom all dressed up like the Stranger Things characters."

(694) Some fans think that Finn would make a good Ben Solo in a Star Wars movie.

(695) Finn said he thought the scariest scene in season of Stranger Things was when Mike jumps off the quarry ledge. He said the Duffer Brothers never told him that Eleven was going to save Mike so he thought his character was being killed off!

(696) Finn is a fan of the movie Under the Skin.

(697) Finn is a fan of a band called The Growlers.

(698) Finn said of Mike Wheeler - "The traits that are my

favorite or that are most relatable about Mike is that he is not afraid of fighting for his opinion. He is very stubborn, but in a great way. He is a leader. He is pretty fearless and he is not afraid of getting his point across. And my favorite trait of his is that he is just kind of a bratty teenager, which I love and I love to play it. And the Duffers love to see me play it because I get flustered in real life and it makes the writing process for them way easier because I write myself into the character. I get to play a version of myself."

(699) Finn is a fan of the singer Jonathan Richman.

(700) Finn finds it amusing that fans want him to play Harry Styles in a One Direction biopic.

(701) You can now buy a Finn Wolfhard pillow throw.

(702) Finn said he loved playing a villain in The Turning.

(703) Finn said he is a bit of a workaholic and should probably take more breaks than he actually does.

(704) Finn says it would fun to play Mike Wheeler again in a reunion in the future years after Stranger Things has ended.

(705) Mike and Eleven in Stranger Things are known as Mileven by fans because of their romance.

(706) In a 2019 article, Men's Health ranked Mike Wheeler as the sixth greatest character in Stranger Things.

(707) Finn's character Trevor seems to be wearing Adidas sneakers in Ghostbusters: Afterlife.

(708) Finn is a fan of the TV show Sex Education.

(709) Finn said one of his most alarming moments came when a taxi he was in was followed by another car. This was presumably a photographer looking to take pictures.

(710) Sputnik Music wrote of Calpurnia's album Scout - 'In the end, then, Scout is neither better nor worse than a thousand other indie-rock debut EP's littering the likes of Bandcamp; the only factor setting Calpurnia aside from these more anonymous bands is the presence of a rising movie and television star in their ranks. The Canadians' debut effort is in no way a bad listen, but neither is it impressive enough to merit anything more than a casually curious couple of spins. In fact, the most lasting feeling it evokes is one of irony – in this case, derived from the fact that the best song Calpurnia ever recorded (infectious rocker Cell) is also the only one not to be present on their debut.'

(711) Finn is said to be a fan of Las Vegas.

(712) Finn said his favourite film genre is comedy. "I love comedy. I've tried so hard to write drama and it's impossible. I can't do it. But when you have a sad life, a sad situation, there are always funny moments. Some people laugh at funerals. In sad situations there is always room for comedic property."

(713) Despite his youth, Finn says he was already familiar with eighties bands The Clash, Joy Division, and New Order before he appeared in Stranger Things.

(714) Finn got a temporary pizza tattoo to celebrate the end of filming on Stranger Things 2.

(715) In a 2019 poll by MoffettNathanson, Stranger Things was voted the second best Netflix show. It was beaten by Orange Is the New Black.

(716) Mike Wheeler ranks fourth in Stranger Things when it comes to the total screen time given to characters in the three completed seasons.

(717) The 2019 film The Goldfinch, which Finn starred in, got very bad reviews.

(718) Finn is a fan of the singer-songwriter Mac Demarco.

(719) On playing a creepy character in The Turning, Finn said -
"Well, it was pretty upsetting for the first week for me, because
I've never really played a character like that before. As the
production went on, I became more involved and it became
way more fun for me."

(720) Bill Hader played the grown-up version of Finn's
character Richie in IT Chapter Two. Finn said - "Bill is a
genius and I certainly wouldn't give him any advice unless he
asked. But we had some great discussions on set when our
days were overlapping. He's obviously a great impressionist
and mimic and I actually can't wait to see the film to see what
he's done with adult Richie."

(721) A strength of Stranger Things is that because you don't
get many episodes the show always feels quite lean and
propulsive. Stranger Things is all about the story moving
forward and creating fresh danger and cliff-hangers.

(722) Mike Wheeler wears Puma sneakers in the first season of
Stranger Things.

(723) Finn likes Apple Earphones.

(724) Stephen King's Carrie, a story about a girl with powerful
telekinetic abilities, was one of but many influences on
Stranger Things.

(725) The Duffer Brothers said that Mike wheeler's name is a
nod to Mikey Walsh in The Goonies.

(726) The kids (now teenagers) in Stranger Things have their
trailers close to one another on the set.

(727) Finn obviously knows Atlanta very well now after
shooting four seasons of Stranger Things there.

(728) Shawn Levy played the Stranger Things score from seasons one and two on the set of (the Stranger Things 3 episode) The Sauna Test to get Finn and the young cast members in the right mood for their confrontation with the possessed Billy Hargrove.

(729) Finn has a Kyocera Contax T2 Camera.

(730) When they made Stranger Things 2, the Duffers and Shawn Levy consulted the producers on Game of Thrones for advice on how to make the set more secure and avoid anyone getting hold of spoilers.

(731) Finn said that his parents think he looks like John Cassavetes' character from Rosemary's Baby.

(732) At the time of writing, the kids in Stranger Things have all been impeccably well behaved and adjusted to fame as well as one might expect. None of them have been involved in any scandals or gone off the rails.

(733) Finn said - "Everyone always asks me, "So what makes you want to do horror?" And I'm like, "I don't know. It's kind of been all a coincidence." It just so happens that the two biggest things I've been in so far are horror, but I hope as my career goes on I can do a bunch of different things."

(734) Finn is a fan of the TV show Big Mouth.

(735) Finn said - "Something Stranger Things had in common with IT was that as big as they are, they feel like indie sets."

(736) Finn has done a photoshoot for Disorder Magazine.

(737) The child extras at the Snow Ball dance finale (where Mike and Eleven kiss) in Stranger Things 2 were not told that they were appearing in Stranger Things and so it came as a nice surprise to them when the penny dropped.

(738) Finn said that he decided he wanted to become an actor after watching the Tobey Maguire Spider-Man movies.

(739) Maya Hawke, who plays Robin in Stranger Things, said she would love Robin to have more scenes with Mike Wheeler because she is good friends with Finn.

(740) Finn said that film sets can be a bit boring sometimes because there is a lot of waiting around and delays sometimes.

(741) Finn said of his research to play Richie in Stephen King's IT - "There's not much research that goes into Richie. You just have to read the character breakdown and it helps a lot to see the difference between the characters in the book, and the miniseries, as well to get a raw take on it. There wasn't much going into it because I had done it a year before so I already knew who Richie was."

(742) In Stranger Things 2, you can see a periodic table on a school classroom wall which contains some elements that hadn't been discovered in 1984.

(743) In Stranger Things 2, we see the Wheeler family using a polaroid camera. These types of cameras were quite a novelty in the 1980s because you didn't have to take your photographs away to be developed. The photo simply rolled out of the camera.

(744) Finn is a fan of milkshakes.

(745) Finn said he has learned a lot about CGI effects and green screen work after making Stranger Things and IT.

(746) Stranger Things has been happily free of scandal and behind the scenes problems in the course of its history and production. You really don't have to go too far at all to encounter television shows (Desperate Housewives, Sex and the City, even, believe it or not, The Golden Girls) which had to deal with some feuding actors who didn't get on at all. Actors

have been fired from TV shows for feuds with producers or scandals in their past. You can list a number of high profile TV shows that had to axe or recast a character because of some offscreen scandal. Stranger Things has, happily, not encountered any of these problems. The cast seem to be one big happy family and there have been no reports of discord or feuds among the cast.

(747) The other cast members in Stranger Things 3 only heard the Dustin and Suzie Neverending Story song duet when the reactions of their character were shot. Their baffled reactions were therefore genuine.

(748) In 1979, 16-year-old child prodigy James Dallas Egbert III vanished from his room at Michigan State University. He was later found in tunnels underneath the university. Egbert, who had mental health problems, later shot himself. His disappearance and later death was all blamed on Dungeons & Dragons. The moral panic over Dungeons & Dragons got so bizarre in the end there were even stories about participants in the game seeking to heighten the experience by having Dungeons & Dragons sessions in caves and underground catacombs and then vanishing - never to be seen again.

These strange (and patently ludicrous) urban legends, along with the real life James Dallas Egbert III incident, inspired a book called Mazes & Monsters which was turned into a 1982 television movies starring a young Tom Hanks. What made the Dungeons & Dragons panic especially silly was that many in the outraged moral minority didn't have the faintest clue what Dungeons & Dragons even was in the first place. The fact that anyone believed your average Dungeons & Dragons player was a Devil worshipping occultist who spent their spare time in caves and catacombs was laughable.

(749) It was widely reported that the cast received hefty pay rises for Stranger Things 3 and that Finn and the kids (or teenagers as they were now) were on $250,000 an episode (a massive increase from the $20,000 an episode the kids were

supposedly on in season one). Millie Bobby Brown's salary though was said to be a mystery. Many entertainment sites speculated that she was now being paid as much as the adult actors like David Harbour (who was said to now be on $350,000 an episode).

(750) Finn is a fan of the film Superbad.

(751) Generous tax incentives in Georgia for screen productions was a factor in why Atlanta was chosen as the production base for Stranger Things.

(752) You don't really see much evidence of the boys in Stranger Things using a computer or playing video games at home. You would expect a science nerd like Dustin to have a home computer and the Wheeler family certainly seem wealthy enough to have a high end (for the time) computer. We did see in season one though that Will Byers seemed quite excited at the thought that one of his Christmas presents might be an Atari.

(753) Finn said he has considered the wet food diet. This is where you eat foods high in water content in order to 'flush' your system.

(754) When asked what his advice was for anyone trying to break into the entertainment industry, Finn said - "Do it yourself. Make your own films and put yourself in them. If you are young and your parents support your dream, get them to help you search for auditions at local film schools or through open casting calls -- but do not do that stuff or Craigslist auditions without an adult. There can be great opportunities on Craigslist but there is creepy stuff there, too."

(755) You can now buy a Finn Wolfhard pillow cover.

(756) Ross Duffer said of casting the kids in Stranger Things - "We had five kids, and we knew that even one [bad child performance] would really hurt the show. Shawn knew that,

we knew that, Netflix knew that. So they the minute they greenlit the show, and at this point we only had one script written at the time, we started a very intensive worldwide search for these kids. When you boil it down, we saw about a thousand kids in total. And when you boil it down, there's so few that can operate at this level that it was instantly clear to everyone which were our kids, and which kids could actually do this show. And I think that, at the end of the day they honestly made the characters more interesting. They did influence the scripts moving forward. They caused us to actually go back and rewrite our pilot script."

(757) Although he finds fame and attention a trifle overbearing, Finn says he does understand it because he has been starstruck himself when he's seen celebrities.

(758) When it comes to music, Finn is a fan of the rock band Wallows.

(759) Finn is a fan of the film The Squid and the Whale.

(760) In May 2017, Finn hosted Strange 80s, a benefit concert to raise funds for artists struggling to afford medicare.

(761) Finn said he would like to be in a Safdie brothers movie. The Safdie brothers are independent filmmakers.

(762) Finn said he has no great interest in being famous but it's just an unavoidable part of being an actor.

(763) IT Chapter Two got more lukewarm reviews than the first movie.

(764) Finn has something in common with Millie Bobby Brown because they both deleted their Twitter.

(765) Finn said The King of Comedy is his favourite Martin Scorsese film.

(766) Although the film didn't do so well, Finn said he enjoyed
acting in The Goldfinch because it was the first time he played
a purely dramatic role in a conventional sort of drama.

(767) Stranger Things never divulges where exactly in Indiana
the town of Hawkins is supposed to be. One of the spin-off
novels seems to suggest it is near Bloomington.

(768) Finn says he has to wear a lot or protective gear when he
goes skateboarding because Netflix (who produce Stranger
Things) would be furious if he got injured.

(769) Finn is a big fan of the 1982 film John Carpenter's The
Thing.

(770) Finn is a fan of the band Guns'n'Roses.

(771) The Wheeler station wagon in Stranger Things 3 is
deliberately similar to the car the Griswold family drive in the
1983 film Vacation.

(772) Stranger Things Ted Wheeler actor Joe Chrest (who
plays Finn's father in the show) said he was surprised by how
much the kids had grown by season three. He noted that Finn
was now as tall as him.

(773) The costume designer Kim Wilcox suggested that the
clothes the boys wear at the Snow Ball dance in Stranger
Things 2 hint at what occupations they might have as adults.

(774) Finn has done a photshoot for Vulkan Magazine.

(775) In the first season of Stranger Things, the Duffer
Brothers admit that entire scenes were shot and designed to
evoke scenes in E.T. the Extra-Terrestrial.

(776) Finn said he was allowed to improvise somewhat as
Richie in IT.

(777) Finn said he has learned a lot from the Duffer Brothers and Shawn Levy working on Stranger Things. "What I've learned from them - and I have learned a lot from Shawn Levy, too - is to be confident in my choices and vision and to make sure you have the best people around you who will execute those choices in the service of the vision. Leaving room for improv and unplanned moments is also really valuable because a good idea can come from anywhere. The Duffers are also incredibly patient and trusting in both their cast and their crew, and that gives everyone else involved the confidence to do their best work and be fearless. It's really a virtuous circle that comes right back to the director."

(778) In the last episode of season one of Stranger Things, the boys play Dungeons & Dragons and comment on how short the campaign was. This is a meta reference to the fact that season one of Stranger Things only consisted of eight episodes.

(779) Finn said it was a bit strange when he graduated high school because his friends were off to college while he was heading back to the world of film and television acting.

(780) Because he spent parts of his childhood in film and television studios and sets, Finn's education was a mix of traditional schools and private tutors.

(781) Finn's favourite Edgar Wright film is Shaun of the Dead.

(782) Stranger Things 2 saw the show move further away from practical effects and become more grand scale and (unavoidably) digital. While you could depict a lone human sized Demogorgon through practical effects for a good portion of the time in season one, it would obviously have been impossible to convey the monstrous gargantuan shapeshifting Mind Flayer through practical effects.

(783) The Duffers said it was very deliberate in season one of Stranger Things the way that the different age groups of characters seem to be in different sorts of movies. "For the

teens they're more in a classic horror film; John Carpenter's stuff like Halloween or Wes Craven's Nightmare on Elm Street. That's where the teens live. For the kids it's more the adventure thing, like The Goonies or Stand by Me. And then the adults are a bit more in the classic Spielberg movies like Close Encounters where they're slowly coming to realise that something extraordinary is happening around them and the sense of wonder that provokes. So that was what we were trying to do. Those are some of the big touchstones for us."

(784) After the Duffers ditched the idea of setting the show in Montauk, everywhere from Texas to the Pacific Northwest was considered as the new backdrop until they settled on Indiana (conveyed in reality by Georgia).

(785) Dan Aykroyd said of granting permission for Ghostbusters uniforms to be worn in Stranger Things - "Well they are just such fans of the Ghostbusters in the show, and it fits perfectly for the timeline of their show. So I believe it was really just a result of how they had linked up our movie with the second season. It just seemed to be a fantastic tie-in and a beautiful nostalgic tie-in as well. So the guys in Stranger Things, essentially they are the Ghostbusters in elementary school."

(786) Finn said it was weird being in a Ghostbusters film because his dad was a big fan of the original.

(787) The kids in Stranger Things say that Gaten Matarazzo is the biggest prankster on the set.

(788) Finn is a fan of Matthew McConaughey.

(789) The kids hiding from the monster in Starcourt Mall in Stranger Things 3 has some obvious similarities to the children trying to hide from the raptors in Jurassic Park.

(790) Patrick Henry Academy at 109 S. Lee St. in Stockbridge was the location for Hawkins High/Middle School in Stranger

Things. This was a real school but one that closed because of a mould problem in the building.

(791) Mike Wheeler has a Teenage Mutant Ninja Turtle action figure in Stranger Things 2 that wasn't released until 1988.

(792) Finn Wolfhard recieved some criticism early on in the history of Stranger Things when he seemed to ignore fan requests for an autograph when entering a building. He was defended by Game of Thrones star Sophie Turner on Twitter. "Damn," she said. "Seeing fully grown adults wait outside the Stranger Things kids' hotels etc , and then abuse them when they don't stop for them is super weird. What adult in their right mind waits for a CHILD outside their hotel and B is then is offended when the CHILD doesn't stop. It doesn't matter if they are an actor, they are kids first. Give them the space they need in order to grow without feeling like they owe anyone anything for living their childhood dreams."

(793) The Duffer Brothers think that Finn has some of his best scenes in Stranger Things 4. They believe he is getting better and better as an actor.

(794) Finn has compared Stranger Things to Harry Potter in that we see the kids grow-up through the course of the story.

(795) The games in the Palace Arcade for Stranger Things 2 were all playable and real. The cast and crew were able to play on the machines between takes.

(796) Finn is a fan of the band Wilco.

(797) Finn is a big fan of the horror film It Follows.

(798) Finn is a fan of Tame Impala. Tame Impala is the psychedelic music project of Australian multi-instrumentalist Kevin Parker.

(799) Finn was nominated for the Teen Choice Awards

breakout star of 2017.

(800) Finn said he never listens to the radio. He is from a generation who just stream or download what they want to listen to.

(801) In Stranger Things 2, you can hear a small burst of the music from Joe Dante's Gremlins when Dustin's pet creature Dart escapes from the boys in the AV room.

(802) When asked if he was closer to the kids in Stranger Things or the kids in IT, Finn said - "I don't know. They're so similar and so different at the same time. I'm close with them in different ways. If it comes down to brass tacks, I guess they're equal."

(803) Dungeons & Dragons fans have suggested that the Mind Flayer in Stranger Things might be a aboleth. Aboleths are tentacled monsters with psionic powers.

(804) The Duffer Brothers said there were no alternatives to the child actors they cast. They felt they had found the only children capable of playing these parts.

(805) Finn is a fan of the animated film Akira. This movie was an influence on the Duffer Brothers and Stranger Things.

(806) Finn said of his character Richie Tozier in IT - "A lot of people have been saying Richie is a fan favorite, and that's really cool. I just did it because I really loved the role and I loved being funny. It was fun for me. I didn't really see the character as a fan favorite."

(807) Finn appears to sometimes wear spectacles when he's at home.

(808) In 2019, Finn grumbled about people who do social media posts on Christmas Day. 'Ugh. Stop sharing every second of your life on social media. Anyways happy holidays.

Why does everyone feel the need to share everything on social media on Christmas? Just spend time with your families.'

(809) They had to use CGI to 'de-age' Finn for his scenes in in IT: Chapter Two. His character Richie had to look the same as in the first film but Finn had obviously changed since then so special effects had to be used.

(810) On the scariest scene in 2017's IT, Finn said the scene where Georgie encounters Pennywise in the drain early on is terrifying to him.

(811) Finn said that when you are an actor it's always more difficult to do a solo scene.

(812) The quarry scenes in Stranger Things were shot at Bellwood Quarry, Atlanta.

(813) David Harbour said the kids in season one of Stranger Things were quite challenging to work with. "I was joking before but it's the farting that goes on with 12-year-olds. The amount of bodily functions they can't control is amazing. It's all kinds of boogers. When you go to work you should not have to deal with someone like — yeah, it was bad. Also now they're growing up, now they're 13, 14 and you know what happens then, right? The hormones, hair growing. It's like weird to watch a human being develop. There are little moments of weirdness. It's great and it's horrible because you want to sort of get your workday done and they're sort of crazy children."

(814) The Stranger Things kids handed out peanut butter and jelly sandwiches to celebrities at the 2016 Emmy awards.

(815) Finn said he would love to make a road-trip movie.

(816) Finn said that PlayStation 1 was his first ever console.

(817) Finn is a fan of Monopoly.

(818) For kids in the early eighties like Mike Wheeler, the video game arcade was still a thing of wonder that offered them a gaming experience they couldn't get on their machines at home.

(819) Finn said that Marmite is one of the most disgusting things he has ever eaten. Marmite is a yeast spread.

(820) Stranger Things 3 had 2,500 special effects shots. This was 500 more than Stranger Things 2.

(821) Finn is a fan of the band Foxygen.

(822) The Stranger Things 3 premiere had a fair theme so Finn and the kids were able to enjoy some funfair rides.

(823) On failing his driving test twice, Finn said - "I failed it twice because I'm an actor, I guess, and dumb. And then I just got so mad at myself that I just didn't do it again."

(824) Finn is a fan of Arcade Fire.

(825) Finn is a fan of Chloë Grace Moretz.

(826) Finn loves the Mandarin Oriental hotel in Paris.

(827) The pitch document for Montauk (eventually to become Stranger Things) was designed to look like a frayed eighties paperback horror novel. The pitch, in order to convey the intended atmosphere and tone of Montauk, included striking still images from the following movies - E.T. the Extra-Terrestrial, Close Encounters of the Third Kind, Altered States, Poltergeist, Hellraiser, Stand By Me, Firestarter, A Nightmare On Elm Street, and Jaws. The influence of these (and many more) films would be plain to see when Stranger Things eventually hit the small screen.

(828) Finn is a fan of Lunar Vacation. This is an Atlanta band.

(829) Of playing Mike Wheeler in Stranger Things, Finn said -
"Playing Mike, I accessed feelings I'd never accessed before. I
emerged a better actor. I want to give myself credit for that,
more than I did at the time. I mean, obviously, there is no
perfect person; there's always work to do. But that's what I
love about acting. You're never perfect."

(830) Finn said that the cast played poker to pass the time
while shooting Stranger Things 4. He said that Charlie Heaton
was the biggest card shark and usually won.

(831) Stranger Things clearly takes some inspiration from
Stephen King's story The Mist (later a movie). The Mist is
about a monster festooned blanket fog which engulfs a small
town after a military experiment goes wrong.

(832) The scene in Stranger Things 3 where Mike tells Will
Byers that it isn't his fault if Will doesn't like girls created
some debate as to whether or not this confirmed that Will
Byers was gay. Noah Schnapp judged the line to be ambiguous
and felt the scene was about the fact that Will was less mature
than his friends and wanted to turn back the clock to the time
before he was trapped in the Upside Down. Finn said they did
several takes and the lines always varied so he didn't think
anything specific was intended.

(833) In season three of Stranger Things, Mike and Eleven
have some M&Ms and you see a few red ones. This is a mistake
because there were no red M&Ms in 1985 thanks to a health
scare about red food dye.

(834) Finn said that Stephen King's Carrie is the scariest book
he has ever read. "It's really, really creepy because it's told
from different perspectives: through one of the teenagers from
high school, from an adult perspective, from the police
investigation. It isn't like that in the movie."

(835) The real exterior for the Wheeler house in Stranger
Things is Piney Wood Lane, East Point, Georgia 30344.

(836) When it comes to music, Finn is a fan of The Lemon Twigs.

(837) On meeting Millie Bobby Brown for the first time, Finn said - "Millie came in, and obviously she's so nice. I'm Canadian, and she's English, and those are two combinations of nice people, which is immediately a good chemistry."

(838) Finn is a fan of The Rolling Stones.

(839) Finn funded his short movie Night Shifts by raising $20,000 through crowdfunding.

(840) in 2020, Finn said of Twitter - "It feels like noise, like a giant air conditioning unit above your bed that's so loud, and then you find the switch to turn it off and you're like, "Oh, nice.""

(841) The Duffer Brothers have said that the 2011 JJ Abrams film Super 8 was an influence on Stranger Things. Super 8 is set in the late 1970s and has a gang of children investigating a strange mystery in their small town.

(842) Finn is a big fan of cookies.

(843) Finn said he doesn't really mind if some people don't like his music. He says he mostly does it becuse it makes him happy.

(844) The horror writer HP Lovecraft is an influence on Stranger Things. Lovecraft's work is full of creatures so indescribably hideous that one look at them would lead to insanity.

(845) Loch Nora, where the kids go trick or treating in Stranger Things 2, is the name of a real place near where the Duffer Brothers grew up in North Carolina.

(846) In the scene in the first episode of Stranger Things 3 (in the car) where a jealous Hopper is trying to get rid of Mike Wheeler, David Harbour had an attack of the giggles and kept flubbing his lines.

(847) Finn is a fan of the horror film The Shining.

(848) The actress Lili Reinhart defended Finn in 2017 when he received criticism for not stopping to sign autographs for fans who were waiting outside of his hotel. "My heart definitely goes out to the Stranger Things cast," she said. "I think it's sickening and disgusting to see someone calling out poor Finn, who's just this young actor, calling him out for being rude because he's not stopping. He's an actor, but he never asked you to take time out of your day to wait for him and his autograph and for a picture with him."

(849) Finn said that the best thing about his fame and success is that it now allows him to decline things he doesn't want to do. He doesn't have to have accept work simply for the money but can pick and choose his projects.

(850) The horror prologue of the doomed scientist in the elevator in the Stranger Things episode The Vanishing of Will Byers was inspired by a scene in Alien 3 where the alien creature pulls a victim up through the ceiling.

(851) Georgia International Horse Park is where many of the woodland scenes in Stranger Things are shot.

(852) There was a slight fear that Finn was starting to get appreciably taller than the other kids by the time Stranger Things 3 rolled around. It was not something though that seemed distractingly glaring onscreen.

(853) Finn said he would love to jam with Paul McCartney.

(854) The Stranger Things cast were allowed to do some free shopping at the Starcourt Mall set near the end of shooting on

season three. The expensive period authentic sneakers were off limits though because they were on loan.

(855) Stranger Things reminded some readers of Dan Simmons' 1991 novel Summer of Night. Summer of Night takes place in a small Illinois town in 1960 and revolves around a gang of boys who are around twelve years-old. The boys love riding their bikes and making dens in the woods. They gradually realise that some mysterious evil has awoken in their town.

(856) David Harbour said Finn and the kids in the cast were rather baffled by the 1980s telephones when they first saw the Stranger Things sets. "In the first season, the biggest thing was the wall telephone with the long cord. I remember all the kids going - What's that?"

(857) Finn is a fan of the singer Jeff Rosenstock.

(858) Finn thinks that luck plays a big part in the film and television world. He was lucky enough to land a part in Stranger Things and the success of the show opened up many doors for him.

(859) Finn loves the Plaza Theatre in Atlanta because it shows old horror movies.

(860) Stranger Things was shot on a digital cinema camera but to achieve the vintage look a layer of scanned film grain was added to the colouring process.

(861) Finn said his family have always had pets and he loves animals.

(862) The first season of Stranger Things has a plot that is rather similar to a Twilight Zone episode called Little Girl Lost. Little Girl Lost is about a girl who becomes trapped in an alternate dimension thanks to a portal in her bedroom.

(863) Finn is a fan of eighties pop group Duran Duran.

(864) Finn is a fan of Jesse Eisenberg.

(865) The music in Stranger Things is heavily influenced by Tangerine Dream. Tangerine Dream is a German electronic music band formed in 1967 by Edgar Froese. They have composed many movie scores - including Legend, Near Dark, The Keep, Firestarter, and Risky Business.

(866) The Stranger Things cast won a SAG Award for Outstanding Performance by an Ensemble in a Drama Series in 2016.

(867) Finn is a fan of merch emblazoned with the logo of independent movie studio Elara.

(868) The newsclip at the end of Stranger Things 3 mentions controversies related to Dungeons & Dragons. In 1982, a young man named Irving Pulling shot himself and his family blamed his obsession with Dungeons & Dragons. An organisation called B.A.D.D. (Bothered About Dungeons & Dragons) and conservative Christian groups tried to get the game banned because they believed it celebrated demonology and witchcraft. The game was banned from a few school libraries in America but most people seemed to feel the campaign against Dungeons & Dragons was silly. The video game Doom and the Harry Potter films would later experience similar moral panics from Christian groups.

(869) On his social media, Stephen King wrote of season one of Stranger Things - "Watching STRANGER THINGS is like watching Steve King's Greatest Hits. I mean that in a good way. STRANGER THINGS is pure fun. A+. Don't miss it."

(870) The Silent Hill video game series was a very obvious influence on the Upside Down in Stranger Things. The town of Silent Hill is a fog bound haunted place where (unseasonal) snow and dust seems to cloud everything in murk and

mystery.

(871) Stranger Things 2 had a budget of $8 million per episode.

(872) The Hawkins Department of Energy building in Stranger Things is really the former Georgia Mental Health Institute (now Emory University Briarcliff Campus, Atlanta). This mental institution closed down years ago and the bleak and functional exterior of the building was perfect for the secret government lab in Stranger Things.

(873) A fan once had a cake delivered Finn's house while he was doing a Livestream. While this was a nice gesture, Finn thought it was a trifle alarming that this fan knew where he lived.

(874) In 2017, Finn made a joke about drinking from a bidet while in France. The French media didn't get the joke though and thought he really had drunk from a bidet!

(875) The Starcourt Mall set in Stranger Things 3 had an operational food court and real hot food was constantly prepared for background extras to eat in scenes.

(876) Finn attended the French premiere of Stranger Things 3 in Paris with Charlie Heaton, Natalia Dyer, and Joe Keery.

(877) EUE/Screen Gems Studios, where Stranger Things is made, is a 10-stage, 33-acre Atlanta studio complex.

(878) Dustin and Suzie singing The Neverending Story song in Stranger Things 3 became something of a mixed blessing for the crew because the kids couldn't stop singing it for days afterwards and it became an 'earworm' for everyone in the production.

(879) The scene in Stranger Things 3 where the kids push Dustin's radio tower aloft in Suzie, Do You Copy? appears to

be based on the World War 2 photograph of the American flag being raised atop Mount Suribachi at the Battle of Iwo Jima.

(880) When Eleven falls into Mike's arms at the end of the sauna battle in the Stranger Things episode The Sauna Test this was not in the script. Millie was genuinely exhausted and Finn caught her. The director Shawn Levy liked this and used it in the episode.

(881) According to reports, Finn made $150,000 for his role in the 2020 horror film The Turning. He was set to make more if the film was a financial success but it didn't do very well in the end.

(882) The Hawkins Department of Energy building in Stranger Things is really the former Georgia Mental Health Institute. This mental institution closed down years ago and the bleak and functional exterior of the building was perfect for the secret government lab in Stranger Things.

(883) Finn said he would love to be in a film with Natalie Portman.

(884) Finn said of Winona Ryder - "She is a total pro and as time goes on, I realize how difficult her job was in season one. She always says to focus on the work and not buy into all the fame and celebrity stuff that comes with being in a popular show. Those are words to live by."

(885) A few days after he received some criticism for not signing autographs for fans outside his hotel, Finn offered an apology on social media.

(886) Finn said it is both cool and weird to be famous.

(887) Finn said if he hadn't become an actor he would liked to have gone to film school.

(888) The villain of Stranger Things 2 is the Mind Flayer - an

unspecified big boss of the Upside Down. The manifestation of the creature is visually inspired by electric storms and volcanoes. The Duffers said that Voldemort in Harry Potter and the stories of Clive Barker were an influence on the Mind Flayer.

(889) Finn is a fan of the activist Greta Thurnberg. He said - "When political leadership is absent or ignorant or compromised, we have to be realistic about the possibilities for change. And when so many adults have their heads so far up their asses that they can't distinguish between fantasy and reality, it's going to be a very tough road."

(890) Finn is a fan of Ariana Grande.

(891) Finn did a Shakespeare camp when he was younger.

(892) Clinical psychologist Dr Renee Carr believes that 'binging' shows like Stranger Things unlocks pleasure receptors in the brain!

(893) Finn has done a photoshoot for At Large Magazine.

(894) Finn Wolfhard said he loved the 'awkward' romance of Mike and Eleven in Stranger Things 3. "I loved the stuff with Eleven in the grocery store aisle and we're sitting down and I'm telling her about love and stuff. And in that scene, I got to explore awkwardness and just be funny. That was fun. And it's the first season where Mike got to flex that muscle and show that he's a weird, funny, awkward dude. And the Duffers loved it and were like, 'Just say more, say more.' And so some of the stuff in that scene was improvised. Mike met her when she didn't even know words. And so there was a barrier there for a while and they are kind of just getting through that barrier."

(896) Finn says that going home to Vancouver keeps him grounded because his friends and family obviously don't treat him like he's a celebrity.

(897) The kids in the Stranger Things 2 cast had their trailers
next to one another and still retained the close bond from
season one. The overnight fame Stranger Things had bestowed
on most of the cast was something that some embraced more
than others. Millie Bobby Brown seemed to be having the time
of her life whereas the very private Natalia Dyer said she had
taken to wearing a hat in public so she wouldn't be recognised.
The cast were experiencing the fringe benefits of being in a hot
TV show. Harbour, Brown, and Charlie Heaton were being
offered movie roles and soon signed up for forthcoming films.
Finn Wolfhard and Joe Keery juggled Stranger Things with
their duties in music bands. The Duffers, David Harbour, and
Winona Ryder all expressed some mild concern at the
tremendous exposure the kids in the cast were recieving -
Brown in particular. They hoped these kids would all avoid the
'child star curse' and grow up to be happy.

(898) The boys in Stranger Things use Telex Headsets on the
ham radio.

(899) Finn said that Raiders of the Lost Ark is one of his
favourite movies.

(900) Finn thought that Eleven and the Byers family moving
out of Hawkins at the end of Stranger Things 3 posed some
interesting questions regarding his character in the show. "I
think it's an interesting thing that if we get a season 4, we can
explore what Mike does. Does he have to make new friends?
Does he have to put himself out there? Does he have to do
things he doesn't necessarily want to do socially? We'll see."

(901) Calpurnia's first single City Boy debuted at No. 23 on
Billboard's Alternative Digital Song Chart and hit No. 1 on
Spotify's Global Viral 50 playlist.

(902) Finn said of Millie Bobby Brown - "I think Millie and I
are very comfortable with ourselves, which is really cool. We
had a bond from the beginning, because I think Millie said one
time that she's crazy and I'm the straight man, but it's sort of

the opposite in Stranger Things because she completely downplays it; she's amazing in it. I think we both knew that we were just doing our jobs and acting."

(903) The children in Stranger Things liken the Upside Down to the Plane of Shadows. The Plane of Shadows is a dimension that exists alongside our own reality. It is there all the time in close proximity but elusive. Although the Duffers are vague about the true nature of the Upside Down we see that actions in our own reality can have a ripple effect in this mysterious Nether. Joyce was able to communicate with Will - albeit with great difficulty and not much clarity. The fact that Will took refuge in the Upside Down version of Castle Byers proves that the real features of Hawkins exist in this strange reality. It is not clear why Will Byers was able to survive the Upside Down and Barb Holland was not. The only explanation is that Will was much better at hiding.

(904) Finn believes in the collective approach to art. "My favorite thing is to have collectives. Even when it comes to filmmaking as well, filmmaking and music and most art in general, I feel like everyone should have the same say. If you're in a collective, I feel like everyone should have the same say."

(905) Stranger Things become a huge phenomenon through word of mouth and positive reviews. Film websites like Badass Digest and Ain't It Cool urged their readers to watch Stranger Things. Stephen King and Steven Spielberg raved about the show. The positive buzz for the show grew and grew. Stranger Things was by some distance the big TV success of the year. The Duffers and Shawn Levy could hardly believe how popular Stranger Things had proved to be. They knew the show was good but they never dreamed it would have such mass appeal. Most people thought that binging all eight episodes of Stranger Things in 2016 was much more fun than watching the latest Hollywood blockbusters. Stranger Things was so good that even David Harbour said he binged the show and got all emotional when Will Byers was rescued at the end.

(906) Despite all the rat carnage in Stranger Things 3, not a single live rat was ever on the set. They were all CGI. That was a relief to Finn given his fear of rats.

(907) Finn said he would quite like to open a club or concert venue one day.

(908) It's safe to say that the Wheelers play a very prominent role in the first season of Stranger Things. The Wheelers would though later take more of a backseat in season two.

(909) Finn said - "I don't take the Internet and social media very seriously. I've grown up around social media but to me what happens on the Internet just doesn't feel real."

(910) Finn was the name of a mythical Irish warrior and folklore hero.

(911) Finn said he doesn't see as much of his Stranger Things co-stars as he would like because they are all so busy.

(912) It took about five months to film the first season of Stranger Things.

(913) Finn is a fan of the French pop band Phoenix.

(914) George A Romero's Day of the Dead hadn't actually been released yet when Stranger Things 3 is set but it is just about possible that Starcourt Mall managed to obtain a special preview screening.

(915) Millie Bobby Brown said she and Finn are just good friends in real life and their romance is strictly confined to their characters in Stranger Things.

(916) Waitresses at the Stranger Things 2 premiere were dressed in special Eggo yellow uniforms.

(917) When Eleven levitates Mike Wheeler's Millennium

Falcon toy in the first season of Stranger Things you can tell it isn't a 1983 period accurate toy because it doesn't have orange stickers to denote the Falcon's engines.

(918) It was costume designer Kimberly Adams who had the clever idea of dressing Millie Bobby Brown (as Eleven) in Finn's Mike Wheeler clothes when she hides out in the basement of the Wheeler house in season one of Stranger Things.

(919) It was humid and sticky in Georgia when they shot the Halloween scenes in Stranger Things 2 so it became something of a challenge to make sure the actors didn't look hot or sweaty in any shots. The children in the cast enjoyed the Halloween scenes. In 2016, after the huge success of season one of Stranger Things, the children in Stranger Things had gone out trick or treating for real but found that no one recognised them.

(920) Finn is a fan of Led Zeppelin.

(921) Before season two of Stranger Things came out there were some stories in the media that Stephen King was going to write the scripts. These stories turned out to be completely bogus.

(922) Walkie-talkies were popular with kids in the eighties, even if they were just talking to each other in the same house from upstairs! They were fun to use.

(923) A lot of people who know Finn think he'll probably end up as a director rather than an actor.

(924) In a poll, Stranger Things came top out of Netflix shows which can be enjoyed the whole family.

(925) Stephen King's Firestarter is a very obvious influence on Stranger Things. This story is about a young girl named Charlie with pyrokinetic powers as a result of her parents

participating in MKUltra style experiments. This book was made into a 1984 film with a very young Drew Barrymore.

(926) Finn said he has learned a lot about acting by working with Natalia Dyer (who plays his sister Nancy Wheeler), Cara Buono (who plays his mother Karen Wheeler) and Winona Ryder in Stranger Things. "Natalia and Cara are such incredible people and amazing actresses. I learned so much about acting from watching each of them and Winona on set. It was incredible to sit back and watch them act. Now it feels like we're all a big family. Natalia is like my big sister and Cara is like my new Mom, it's crazy. And watching Winona in scenes was so surreal and I learned so much from her."

(927) Finn is a fan of The Flaming Lips.

(928) Finn Wolfhard said the Dustin/Suzie NeverEnding Story song duet is the scene in Stranger Things 3 he likes the most.

(929) The music website NME (New Musical Express) ranked Finn's former group Calpurnia as the best of the (at the time) four bands that Stranger Things cast members have been part of.

(930) Finn is a fan of the classic Roman Polanski horror film Rosemary's Baby.

(931) It was very warm and humid in Georgia when they shot the Halloween scenes for Stranger Things 2. Although the scenes were supposed to depict autumn and early winter, the cast were very hot.

(932) Finn said that one day he will read Stephen King's IT but for now he just doesn't have the time.

(933) Finn said he would like to play the young John Lennon in a biopic.

(934) Finn thinks that Mike Wheeler was more mature in

Stranger Things 3. "In a lot of ways through season 3, a lot of the characters have grown and Mike has grown a lot this third season. He learns a valuable lesson about friendship and not having control over situations and letting things just happen and that people will come and go in his life."

(935) Hasbro released a Stranger Things Dungeons & Dragons Starter Set. In the game you can embark on a Dungeons & Dragons adventure and hunt for the Thessalhydra in a campaign "created" by Mike Wheeler.

(936) The Duffer Brothers say the kids in Stranger Things swear much more in real life than they do in the show!

(937) Although it is sometimes suggested that the first season of Stranger Things operated on a modest budget this is not really true. At $6 million an episode, the first season cost around $50 million. While this is modest compared to big Hollywood movie blockbusters, $6 million an episode is fairly high end for a TV show - especially a brand new one with no track record to speak of.

(938) There is no official product placement in Stranger Things 3 (in that no one paid Netflix to get their products and brands in the show) but brands like 7-Up, Casio, Reebok, Burger King, and many others are very visible. It is estimated that these companies would have had to pay tens of millions of dollars to get their brands in the show if an official product placement policy had been in place. One official tie-in that did occur after the release of season three came with the reintroduction of a Stranger Things themed New Coke. The general consensus on New Coke is that is that it simply tastes sweeter than the original Coca-Cola. Many people seem to prefer the slight acid citrus bite of the original rather than the more syrupy New Coke.

(939) In season one of Stranger Things there was an even split between practical and CG special effects. Season three, by contrast, was nearly all CGI.

(940) The television set in the Wheeler house that Mike proudly shows Eleven in season one of Stranger Things is a 22-inch Mitsubishi.

(941) On the unavoidable delay to Stranger Things 4 due to COVID, Finn said that it was a blessing in disguise because it allowed more time for the scripts to be refined and completed.

(942) Finn said that because he wants to be a director one day that when he's on a set as an actor he tries to study the technical aspects that go into making a movie or TV show.

(943) When Finn received criticism in 2017 for not stopping to pose for pictures with fans outside his hotel, he was defended by his Stranger Things co-star Shannon Purser (who played Barb Holland in season one). Purser said - "No actor is under any obligation to stop for anyone. Finn is an incredibly kind human. But he's human and he needs breaks too. From one big sister to the world, don't you DARE make young actors feel guilty or indebted to you because they couldn't say hi."

(944) Stranger Things fan theories really started to go haywire around the time of season two. The theories are always fun to read even if most of them have no validity when it comes to what the Duffers actually intended or might be planning. The most far out theories included the suggestion that the Demogorgon was Will Byers from the future. If this sounds unlikely then even more unlikely was the theory that the Mind Flayer was an evil Upside Down version of Barb. The theory that the Upside Down is a version of Hawkins ruined by nuclear war is a popular (and slightly more plausible) theory. In this theory, the Demogorgons would be humans who had evolved and mutated in the fallout. The most obvious problem with this theory is that it doesn't explain what the Mind Flayer might be or where that came from.

(945) Finn said he is lucky because he has always known what he has wanted to do with his life and has been able to

accomplish this.

(946) Finn said that one thing he loves about Stranger Things is that there are obviously no scenes involving cell phones.

(947) Finn is a fan of the movie Little Miss Sunshine.

(948) The Duffer Brothers said it was planned right from the start that Stranger Things 2 would end at the Snow Ball.

(949) The Stranger Things kids watched the Superbowl teaser for Stranger Things 2 together.

(950) The 'binge' option with Stranger Things was an integral part of its appeal and success. When a new season arrives, viewers can watch all of the episodes as quickly as they want. This is why so many episodes of Stranger Things end with a cliff-hanger. There is no frustration for the viewer because you don't have to wait a week to see what happens next. The fact that episode titles in Stranger Things are preceded by a chapter number is no gimmick. Each episode is designed to be like a chapter in a book that has you eager to turn the page (or cue up the next episode in this case). Shawn Levy has said that he would be disappointed if anyone DIDN'T binge Stranger Things. That's exactly what it was designed for.

(951) Finn is a fan of the band White Reaper.

(952) In his Calpurnia days, Finn said that it did bother him slightly if people only turned up to concerts because he was Mike from Stranger Things.

(953) Finn said of the contrast between his characters in Stranger Things and Stephen King's IT that Richie is super annoying while Mike is more of a leader.

(954) Finn said he wrote a lot of songs and scripts during the COVID quarantines.

(955) Finn is a fan of the Mel Brooks film Young Frankenstein.

(956) Among the board games you can see in the Wheeler basement in season one of Stranger Things are Upwords and Score Four.

(957) Finn thinks he is good at reading people.

(958) Finn is a big fan of the Angry Video Game Nerd reviews on the YouTube channel Cinemassacre.

(959) Finn says that Wolfhard means heart of the wolf in German.

(960) Finn is the nephew of the actor Hadley Kay. Hadley was a child actor himself and appeared in films like Superman II.

(961) Finn thinks it is pure coincidence that he's been cast in so many retro period pieces.

(962) Finn said he would love Mike Wheeler to have more scenes with Dustin and Steve in Stranger Things.

(963) Finn is a fan of (the band) Twin Peaks.

(964) Costume designer Amy Parris says that in Stranger Things 3 they tried to make Mike Wheeler look more mature.

(965) Among the Stranger Things themed food items now available is a 'I Dump Your Ass' chocolate bar featuring Eleven and Mike on the wrapping.

(966) Finn and the boys had a fit of the giggles shooting the Dungeons & Dragons scene that begins the first season of Stranger Things.

(967) Finn described making IT: Chapter Two and Stranger Things 3 at the same time as "super tiring and stressful, but really rewarding at the same time."

(968) Finn says it's always embarrassing as an actor when you fluff some lines and have to do another take.

(969) The Wheeler home, where Eleven secretly lives in the basement after the boys find her in the woods in season one of Stranger Things, was loosely inspired by the house in Tobe Hooper's 1982 film Poltergeist.

(970) Ross Duffer says he knew that Stranger Things would not have worked if they didn't find the right child actors.

(971) The costume designer on Stranger Things said Finn and the other kids never brought their high fashion attitudes onto the set and were always happy to wear what their characters were given. "They don't bring in their high fashion wants into the room because they know that's not what their characters are about. They're very professional. I've worked with a lot of very young actors in my career and these are some of the most talented, most fun, most professional actors I've ever worked with — at any age."

(972) Aestheticmagazinetoronto.com wrote of Calpurnia's album Scout - 'The Calpurnia sound is mellow, groovy and at times quirky. Images of summer in the city come to mind. This album can be likened to an oil painting with a strong sense of composition where certain colours of the palette need refining. With a solid start, Calpurnia has the tools to keep this momentum going. One thing is for certain, this band knows their sound.'

(973) Of the original 1984 Ghostbusters film, Finn Wolfhard said he watched it when he was very young. He said it was quite surreal to be cast in a Ghostbusters after his Stranger Things character Mike Wheeler did some Ghostbusters cosplay in season two.

(974) Will Byers tells Mike in Stranger Things 2 that his connection to the Upside Down is like a View-Master. View-

Master was a popular toy in the eighties. It was essentially like 3-D goggles into which you put photographic slides to view. The slides you purchased for the View-Master were usually television and film tie-ins like the Muppets or the latest Hollywood blockbusters.

(975) A number of actors (including Finn) in Stranger Things have said that Duffer Brothers allow them to have a lot of input into the evolution of their characters.

(976) Finn said he found it slightly easier to play Richie Tozier in IT than Mike Wheeler in Stranger Things.

(977) The kids in the Stranger Things cast think that the mall they used to film season three might be haunted.

(978) The plot of Stranger Things 3 reminded some movie buffs of the 1998 sci-fi film The Faculty.

(979) Finn said he has always been interested in horror and the supernatural.

(980) Finn is a fan of the late comedian Andy Kaufman.

(981) Because he has failed his driving test twice, Finn said he wasn't allowed to drive the famous Ecto-1 car in Ghostbusters: Afterlife.

(982) In 2018 a Kickstarter campaign was created to bring back the classic Dungeons & Dragons figurines seen in Stranger Things.

(983) The first season of Stranger Things conformed to the blueprint in the pitch bible of rooting the horror and story in science and some sort of reality. MKUltra and the Department of Energy were not fiction but real. Stranger Things used the fact that government projects and departments like this are understandably secretive to take artistic licence and incorporate them into a science fiction horror story. In real

life, the Department of Energy is tasked with managing the
United States' nuclear infrastructure and energy policy. The
Department of Energy also funds scientific research. After the
first season of Stranger Things came out, a former employee at
the Department of Energy wrote an article about the show and
pointed out all the important and necessary tasks that the
DOE does for the safety of the American public. The Duffers
were very amused by this intervention. They thought it was
funny that those connected to the DOE felt it necessary to
inform the public that they were not involved in the
development of super powered children or opening portals to
other dimensions.

(984) Finn's band the Aubreys are named after his childhood
cat Aubrey.

(985) In an episode of The Simpsons, Homer watched a
Stranger Things parody called Odder Stuff.

(986) Finn can play the harmonica.

(987) Finn said - "I wouldn't call myself a spiritual person. I go
to church sometimes. But I definitely believe in some sort of
supernatural elements in the universe."

(988) Finn said he bonded very quickly with the other boys in
the cast of Stranger Things. He said it immediately felt as if
they had all known each other for months.

(989) In 2017, Finn donated the proceeds from merchandise
connected to him to spreading awareness and acceptance for
autism.

(990) According to the votes on Ranker, the three best
episodes of Stranger Things are The Battle of Starcourt, The
Upside Down, and The Gate.

(991) Finn said he was surprised when Stranger Things
became a fairly immediate hit. He said he was confident that

people would enjoy the show but he had no idea it would become such an instant phenomenon.

(992) Finn is a fan of the rock band SWMRS.

(993) You can now buy a Mike Wheeler Funko Pop.

(994) Finn said his kiss with Millie Bobby Brown in season one of Stranger Things wasn't his first kiss. Millie teased him about this and said it probably was his first kiss.

(995) Finn said that Trick or Treat, Freak is his favourite Stranger Things episode out of the first two seasons.

(996) The Duffer Brothers said that when Finn did his first Stranger Things audition they spent most of the time talking about 80s movies with him.

(997) Finn is a fan of Drew Barrymore.

(998) Finn is a big fan of the 1993 film Dazed and Confused.

(999) Finn says that overnight fame has been a strange experience.

(1000) Finn said - "At the end of the road, I want to look back and say I sat in a room with all of my friends and laughed really hard and we all made something together and we did it over and over and over again. That's what I want to do for the rest of my life."

Other Books by Mera Wolfe

1000 Millie Bobby Brown Facts

1000 Harry Potter Facts

1000 Billie Eilish Facts

1000 Ariana Grande Facts

1000 Friends Facts

1000 Gatan Matarazzo Facts